"As I read this book, it was so evident that it comes from a wise and compassionate pastor. We are reminded that we were made for a new world that is coming, that the best is yet to be. The book is hopeful but realistic, challenging but balanced. I am confident that many readers will be encouraged and convicted by this gem of a book."
Professor Thomas R. Schreiner, Professor of New Testament Interpretation at The Southern Baptist Theological Seminary, Louisville; author of "The King In His Beauty"

"In this book, Stephen Witmer lifts up our eyes to see beyond the 'now' that presses in on us to what is eternal. More than that, he lifts up our eyes to see the eternal God in the magnificence of his redeeming purposes. What encouragement this brings to the spiritually weary and what challenge it brings to those tempted to fall asleep amid the buzz and plenty of our modern world! This treatment of deep, biblical themes is fresh, pastoral, and stimulating. Highly commended."
Professor David F. Wells, Distinguished Research Professor at Gordon-Conwell Theological Seminary; author of "God In The Whirlwind"

"A previous generation sometimes focused so much on the future that they seemed to forget that eternity begins in the here and now. But today's generation often focuses so much on the present world that we can neglect the coming reality of the new heavens and earth. For this reason, I am thankful for this wise book by Stephen Witmer. He knows how to communicate the biblical story of eternity—both present and future—in a winsome, compelling, and genuinely helpful way. May the Lord stir in all of us restless patience as we lean forward toward eternity with the help of this excellent book."
Justin Taylor, blogger at Between Two Worlds; co-author of "The Final Days of Jesus"

"What Stephen Witmer has accomplished here is akin to enjoying a coffee with a new friend as he brilliantly and winsomely shares the secret of the universe with you. Full of both passion and clarity, *Eternity Changes Everything* invites us and helps us to share God's vision for the world and the people in it in view of the glory of Christ's kingdom."
Jared Wilson, Pastor of Middletown Springs Community Church, Middletown Springs, Vermont; author of "Gospel Wakefulness"

"Stephen Witmer does us a great service by counseling real impatience and patient endurance in the Christian life between the first and second comings of Jesus Christ. Whatever your circumstances, this book will fill you with longing for Jesus' return."
Collin Hansen, Editorial Director at The Gospel Coalition; co-author of "A God-Sized Vision"

"If I knew the future, then surely that would affect every minute of the present. But I do know the future. Christians are going to live day after day in a gloriously renewed creation with our Saviour. Yet this certain future has so little impact on how I live most days—so Christ put Stephen Witmer's book in front of me. Reading it reminded me of my future and immediately and hugely shifted my outlook on the present. I have already recommended this book and will keep doing so. It is a readable, simple, hopeful and deep book on a crucial topic. It will change our lives, churches and evangelism."
John Hindley, Pastor of BroadGrace, Norfolk, UK; author of "Serving Without Sinking"

"For a book dealing with the issue of eternity, this is definitely a quick read. What makes it so engaging is that Stephen comes across as so likeable, and has a great illustration on almost every page. A hope-filled, encouraging gem of a book. I loved it."
Mez McConnell, Senior Pastor of Niddrie Community Church, Edinburgh, Scotland, and Director of 20Schemes; author of "Is There Anybody Out There?"

"*Eternity Changes Everything* shows us how heavenly ideas can come down right into the nooks and crannies of everyday life—parenting, suffering, work, and more. Stephen makes you lean forward to heaven in holy restlessness and enduring patience. Every truth he explains he applies to reality. Here is a writer who pastors, and a pastor who thinks. This is theology that breathes and sings. I can't wait for more Stephen Witmer!"
Jonathan Dodson, Lead Pastor at City Life Church, Austin, Texas; author of "Gospel-Centered Discipleship"

"For some, the future looms so large that this present world holds no importance. For others, the present is so critical that God's promised future holds little significance. For Stephen Witmer and his readers, the present and the future are vitally connected. *Eternity Changes Everything* provides necessary perspective and practical guidance for walking the tightrope of the already and not yet. Heartily recommended."
Stephen T. Um, Senior Minister of Citylife Presbyterian Church, Boston, Massachusetts; author of "Why Cities Matter"

"Hope has fallen on hard times in our cynical, I-want-it-now generation. Even within the church, many are settling for a pathetic best life now, rather than holding out for a life that offers a foretaste of the infinitely better life to come. Witmer is a superb biblical scholar with a pastor's heart, so on every page there are fresh insights and much-needed spiritual remedies."
Gordon P. Hugenberger, Senior Minister, Park Street Church, Boston, Massachusetts

Surely goodness + mercy shall follow me all the days of my life; and I shall dwell in the house of the Lord forever – Ps. 23:6

Eternity changes everything

How to live now in the light of your future

Stephen Witmer

Eternity changes everything: *How to live now in the light of your future*
© Stephen Witmer/The Good Book Company, 2014

Published by
The Good Book Company
Tel (UK): 0333 123 0880;
International: +44 (0) 208 942 0880
Email: info@thegoodbook.co.uk

Websites:
US & Canada: www.thegoodbook.com
UK: www.thegoodbook.co.uk
Australia: www.thegoodbook.com.au
New Zealand: www.thegoodbook.co.nz

ISBN: 9781909559912

Printed in the UK
Design by André Parker

Contents

To my wife Emma, our children Samuel, Annie and Henry,
and our church family at Pepperell Christian Fellowship.
I'm glad to be living with you toward the new creation.

1. Your future in your present

Vacations are great. It's wonderful to unplug and unwind, relax and recharge away from normal responsibilities. I love going on vacation. Who doesn't?!

But I also love the last couple weeks before the vacation. Even though nothing changes externally—even though my schedule and responsibilities stay the same—it usually feels to me as though my vacation has partially begun already. It's my "pre-vacation vacation"—and it makes a big difference. I tend to be an all-around nicer guy. I'm more relaxed and forgiving toward other people. Tough stuff rolls more easily off my back because, hey, 16 days from now I'll be lying on my back, on a beach, in the sun.

To enjoy my pre-vacation vacation, I just need to know two things about the vacation itself:

(1) It will be great when I get there.

(2) Nothing will stop me from getting there.

Obviously, the first point is crucial. If I learn that the reason I got the heavily discounted and non-refundable deal on our hotel is that it sits next door to a landfill, I'll spend my last couple of pre-vacation weeks frantically researching local wind patterns, rather than feeling excited. Or if I decided in a rash moment that hiking a 100-mile forest trail would be a good challenge for my wife and me—and forgot to consult my wife—I'll spend the last couple of pre-vacation weeks working up my courage to tell her, rather than feeling excited. ("That's correct, there are no hot showers on the trail... but, on the bright side, it's supposed to rain most of the week! Bring soap!")

And the second point is equally crucial. It doesn't matter how good my destination is if I may never get there. The remote, South Pacific island paradise that can be reached only by means of that World War II-era, island-hopping airplane with rusty bolts and an inebriated pilot, just started sounding like a paradise that is probably out of reach. I remember as a boy how the thrill of our upcoming family vacation was diminished when we heard a winter storm was blowing in. Excitement about leaving was replaced with worry about getting stuck at home, or halfway there.

Our view of the future—whether it's our vacation, our career, our health, or anything else—affects how we feel, and how we act, in the present. The future is an unruly thing. It refuses to stay quietly in its place. It's always lurching into the present—the scary job interview gives us sweaty palms days in advance, or the promise of summer vacation helps us survive the last three weeks of school. We're constantly experiencing the pain and joy and anxiety and delight and fear of future events before we experience the actual events. It's the way we're wired. We are always living toward the future, and the future is always reaching back toward us. It often gets to us (in our thoughts and feelings) before we get to it (in our actual experience).

Our view of our future in this life affects how we live. As we'll see in this book, that is true also of our future beyond this life.

So, what do you think your future beyond this life is? How sure are you about your answer? Where will you be in two hundred years?

One answer is: *nowhere*. The apostle Paul, writing to one of the first churches in the city of Corinth in Greece, put it bluntly:

> If the dead are not raised, "Let us eat and drink, for tomorrow we die." (1 Corinthians 15 v 32)

If our future is nothingness, then let's grab everything we can now. If we're heading for non-existence, all that matters is right now, doing what looks and feels and seems to make us happiest. Let's eat and drink all we can.

That wasn't Paul's own attitude, though. In another one of his letters, he wrote:

> For to me, to live is Christ and to die is gain.
>
> (Philippians 1 v 21)

That's the other end of the spectrum of views about the future. Paul thinks that what lies beyond death is way better than anything in his present. It is gain, because he will experience even more of Christ than he presently enjoys in this life. Everything we read about Paul in the New Testament shows that this conviction about the future allowed him to happily give up anything now, because he was sure he was heading for everything after death.

I don't think there's nothing beyond death, that this is all there is. But neither do I always live with Paul's unshakeable conviction of a certain, perfect future. In fact, I think most of us live between those two extremes—not so certain there's nothing beyond death that we never worry about it, but not so certain there's perfection beyond death that we never worry about now. We worry about what's coming after death, and whether, if it is really great, we'll actually be there; and we find ourselves focusing everything on now, even though we have a vague sense that eternity might be more important.

And that suggests that we're not totally sure about where we're heading in our eternal future. We're not confident it's great; and/or we're not confident we'll get there. It shows in the way we think, feel and act today.

So this book is about the *future*. Chapters Two and Three are all about where this world is heading—I hope you'll find them tremendously exciting.

And this book is about *our* future. Chapters Four and Five are about how we can know for sure where we are heading—I hope you'll find them really reassuring.

And, because those chapters are about our future, the rest of the book is about our *present*—about the difference knowing our future makes to how we view our lives, and live our lives, right now. I hope you'll find the second half of this book both thrilling and transforming.

The future matters. Eternity changes everything. Let's go there now.

2. Everything new

How do you think this world will end? With a bang? Or a fizzle? Or something in between? Will our worst Hollywood-style nightmares come true—asteroid impact, catastrophic climate change, nuclear war, extraterrestrial invasion, or global pandemic? Will you and I be there to see the end when it comes, or will we be long gone by then?

Or will the world perhaps not end at all? Will there instead be a great breakthrough, a technological innovation that preserves and enhances life, and restricts all those catastrophic endings to the plotlines of blockbuster films? Will life here endure forever, getting better and better?

What's your best guess? Because really, it's all just guess-work, isn't it?

Well, actually, no, it's not! God could have left us guessing about the ultimate future of this world. But remarkably, he hasn't. Instead, he has answered our questions. Even more remarkably, the future he reveals to us is far better than anything we could have imagined. Here it is:

> Then I saw "a new heaven and a new earth," for the first
> heaven and the first earth had passed away, and there was
> no longer any sea. I saw the Holy City, the new Jerusalem,

coming down out of heaven from God, prepared as a bride
beautifully dressed for her husband. And I heard a loud voice
from the throne saying, "Look! God's dwelling-place is now
among the people, and he will dwell with them. They will be
his people, and God himself will be with them and be their
God. 'He will wipe every tear from their eyes. There will be
no more death' or mourning or crying or pain, for the old
order of things has passed away."   (Revelation 21 v 1-4)

This is a vision of the world's future given to one of Jesus'
disciples, John, late in his life. But it's not just the wishful
thinking of an aged disciple:

He who was seated on the throne said, "I am making
everything new!" Then he said, "Write this down, for these
words are trustworthy and true." (v 5)

The promise comes from "the throne," which symbolizes God's
sovereign rule. The God who stands behind his promise is the
One who sits upon his throne. No one can stop him. His words
are "trustworthy and true." The vision is certain.

And what a beautiful vision it is! Hollywood tends to offer
us an apocalyptic vision of lonely, desperate survivors. But
John sees a city filled with people who belong to God. In this
community, nothing goes wrong. There's no chaos (that's what
"sea" is an image of—and there will be "no longer any sea").
All residents love one another perfectly. There's no need for
police officers, security cameras, law courts, hospitals, homeless
shelters, or prisons. It's the perfect neighborhood. Wouldn't you
like to settle down here?

This isn't a burned-out husk of an earth; it is a beautiful
place to live. John describes this beauty poetically by picturing
the "new Jerusalem" as "a bride beautifully dressed for her
husband." I love this image. Because I'm a minister, I get the

best seat in the house whenever I perform a wedding. I stand at the front with the groom and his friends. As the music for the bride's entrance begins, I get to look over the groom's shoulder to the back of the room, and I get to see the groom's face as he spots his wife-to-be coming to meet him. Is there any greater beauty than a bride about to walk down the aisle? She's vibrant with nervous joy, smiling, crying, laughing. Her hair is styled, her nails painted, she's wearing a gorgeous dress. And the best part is that she's made herself beautiful as a gift for her soon-to-be-husband.

The ultimate future of this world will not be decay, disorder, or disaster. In the end, this world will be beautiful as a bride.

The future of this world is certain and it is beautiful. But above all, it is new. When God sums up the meaning of John's vision, he says: "I am making everything new" (v 5). That word "new" is used four times in this short passage, because it's the main idea we're meant to take away. John sees a new heaven and a new earth and a new Jerusalem as God makes everything new. But what exactly does newness mean? Let's look more closely at John's vision in order to see three features of the newness of the future world.

Newness: some things are removed

Some things disappear forever:

> Then I saw "a new heaven and a new earth," for the first heaven and the first earth had passed away, and there was no longer any sea ... "He will wipe every tear from their eyes. There will be no more death" or mourning or crying or pain, for the old order of things has passed away. (v 1, 4)

There's a lot of "passing away" going on here! Part of newness is getting rid of the old.

That's because, as the pastor and author Jonathan Dodson puts it, this world is really "old" in terms of its spiritual state. It is sore in the joints, bowed in the back, sickly and decrepit. This tottering world is broken and flawed and full of sadness and death wherever we turn. You don't need to live long in it to sense that it's not what it's supposed to be, or what we would like it to be. We experience its old age every day. Another religious zealot explodes himself, killing innocent bystanders. Old age. Another government official exploits his office for personal gain. Old age. I watch my friends' marriage disintegrate into infidelity and heartache. Old age. I lose my temper at my kids. Old age. Promises are broken, feelings hurt, jobs lost, sicknesses spread, sad farewells made. Old. Old. Old.

I can feel this world's decrepit age in the messy, gasping sobs of my friend who hates his own actions but feels unable to stop them. I can see it in the eyes of a church member whose crippling anxiety disorder keeps her from church. I can hear it through the pane of prison glass in the voice of the sex offender I visit in prison. It's everywhere.

Now look at the future: "the old order of things has passed away." Death, tears, mourning, and pain—*gone* (v 4). Our worst experiences will disappear and our best experiences will improve. In this life, even in our moments of keenest pleasure, we're aware deep down that death can snatch away what we enjoy. Or we're sad about the person who is missing from our happy scene. When death dies, we'll fully enjoy the things we love, with people we love, knowing they will never end! Think of the most discouraging pains, humiliations, weaknesses, and inconveniences you've experienced in this world. Now imagine them completely removed, forever. Consider your most entangling flaws, the ones that keep tripping you up. They will pass away. The old and broken will be gone. What remains will be new and flawless.

Newness: some things remain

Perhaps surprisingly, though, John does not mean that everything will pass away. Granted, it might seem as though God's plan is to destroy this world, create a totally new one, and take his people there. After all, John refers to a new heaven and a new earth, and we often use the word new to mean "different." If I buy a new car, it's a totally different car than the one I had before. Surely, God is going to junk this entire world and start over with a new one?

Here's where it's important to read individual passages of the Bible within the context of all the Bible. We need to set John's vision alongside other passages that describe God's future plans for this world. For instance, Paul speaks of the present creation being "liberated" from slavery to decay and brought into "glorious freedom" (Romans 8 v 21). This is a powerful image, with a clear implication. When a slave is freed from bondage, he's a "new" person in that he's now a free man— but he's still the same person. Since God's plan is to "liberate" this world, we should expect that, even with massive changes and improvements, the new world will be the same world. The "newness" of Revelation 21 is a great renovation of this earth, rather than a total replacement of it.

We're actually quite used to this type of newness. Not long ago, my children found a caterpillar in our back yard, named him Patrick, and brought him inside to live in our house in hopes that he would change into a glorious butterfly (sadly, he died a premature death). When a caterpillar disappears into a cocoon and emerges as a butterfly, the caterpillar has "passed away." But actually, as the pastor John Piper has pointed out, only certain features of the caterpillar have passed away. The butterfly that emerges from the cocoon is a renewed, improved version of the caterpillar, rather than a different creature altogether.

We see the same thing at the end of the Gospels, after Jesus has risen from the dead. It's clear that his resurrection body was a renewed, transformed body. He could walk through walls (John 20 v 26)! At times he was not recognized even by his closest friends (John 21 v 4). But it's equally clear that Jesus' resurrection body was not totally different from the body he possessed before he died, because it still had nail marks from the cross (John 20 v 27). Jesus' resurrection body was a renewal of his former body, not a replacement. Similarly, the new earth will be a renewed and purified version of this present earth.

This world on which we walk will one day be magnificent beyond imagining. And it will be this world, perfected.

This helps us get excited about the future—because we can already see glimmers of this world's future in its present. I remember waking one morning several years ago in a cottage on the Antrim Coast of Northern Ireland and walking to a tiny village perched on the edge of the Irish Sea. The sun was rising over vivid green fields, sheep grazing, the brisk wind gusting in my face, and I could see the wild ocean away on my left. I was so invigorated and delighted I began jumping up and down. I couldn't think what else to do!

You may never have jumped up and down... but has this world ever taken your breath away? By telling us that the new creation is the renewal of this one, God invites us to imagine what he has in store—to imagine the beauty of this world multiplied one thousand times, and all its badness removed.

Let's untether our imaginations and let them soar. Think of the keenest pleasures you've experienced in this world. Now imagine them heightened and purified and prolonged for ever. Colors will be more vivid, jokes funnier, and the taste of food richer. Somehow a steak will be more a steak. A flower will be more a flower. A friend will be more a friend. What will it be like to enjoy friendship without even a hint of envy or anger or disappointment, without secrets and insecurities... for ever? ("Remember that time three million years ago when you helped me with...!") How good will that be? Honestly, we've enjoyed only the faintest hints of real friendship in this life.

Or think of a time when you experienced a brand new pleasure you'd never known. Remember your first taste of a favorite food (I was in my twenties before I ever had really good pork barbecue) or your first kiss (I'm not saying how old I was for that one). Didn't life seem to expand a bit with those discoveries? Didn't you feel as if your world got a little bigger? Now imagine a fresh and delightful discovery of some new, pure pleasure... every day... forever. Our lives will grow and grow.

In this life, we're experiencing only a fraction of true life. We're like the little kid who bangs away on three piano keys and thinks he's playing the piano. The new creation is God's invitation to enjoy the rest of the keyboard. We're like the color-blind man who gasps in delight at a rainbow. The new creation is God's invitation to enjoy the rest of the spectrum.

At the end of C.S. Lewis' *The Last Battle,* the last in his books based in the land of Narnia, the unicorn gallops wildly into the new earth, saying:

> I have come home at last! This is my real country! I belong here. This is the land I have been looking for all my life,

though I never knew it till now. The reason why we loved the old Narnia is that it sometimes looked a little like this.

In the new creation, shadows will give way to reality, and every imperfection will become perfect. If this all sounds really good to you, it's because God intends it to. He designed you for this place. What water is to a fish, what a nest is to a bird, what a green pasture is to a horse, this place is to you. It's your native element. It's your home.

Newness: some things return

In the future, some things will be removed; some things will remain; and some things will return. In the first book of the Bible, Genesis, we're taken back to the beginning of this world, when Adam and Eve ruled over a flawless creation. As we read the last chapter of the last book of the Bible, and are taken forward to the future, we see that the world's newness is in part a return to the goodness of that first world:

> Then the angel showed me the river of the water of life, as clear as crystal, flowing from the throne of God and of the Lamb down the middle of the great street of the city. On each side of the river stood the tree of life, bearing twelve crops of fruit, yielding its fruit every month. And the leaves of the tree are for the healing of the nations. No longer will there be any curse.   (Revelation 22 v 1-3)

All this newness and beauty recalls the original, perfect creation, when God first placed Adam and Eve in the Garden of Eden. The "river of the water of life" flowing from God's throne recalls the river that flowed out of Eden (Genesis 2 v 10-14). The tree of life growing on each side of the river recalls the tree of life that grew in Eden (Genesis 2 v 9). But the first humans lost all this when they chose to sin, to reject God and rule the world themselves. They came under the "curse" of a world far less good than it was designed to be. But this isn't the end of the story. The precious gifts lost through human sin will be fully reclaimed in the new creation. John's vision shows us that the oldness of this fallen world will finally return to beautiful newness. The curse will be lifted.

Better than heaven

All this means that when we die and go to heaven, we won't be fully satisfied with it—nor should we be. *There's somewhere better than heaven.* Pause. What did he just say? Yes, that's right. Heaven is not as good as it gets.

When Christians die, we go immediately to heaven while our bodies remain on earth (2 Corinthians 5 v 8). Heaven will be a wonderful experience. We'll enjoy sharing in the perfectly loving relationship of God the Father, his risen Son, and his Holy Spirit, and being reunited with loved ones who have died trusting in Jesus.

But as good as this is, heaven is not our best or final destination. If we could see into the present heaven and catch a glimpse of what's happening there, what would we see? We would see God's people waiting for something even better:

> I saw under the altar [in God's heavenly throneroom] the souls of those who had been slain because of the word of God and the testimony they had maintained. They called out in a loud voice, "How long, Sovereign Lord, holy and true, until you judge the inhabitants of the earth and avenge our blood?" Then each of them was given a white robe, and they were told to wait a little longer. (Revelation 6 v 9-11)

Christians in heaven are waiting. To live in heaven now is to experience unimaginable joy while longing for something even better: God's return, the arrival of justice, and the bringing of the new creation. What an amazing indication of the beauty of the new creation: it's better than heaven! This is the future of our world!

And even that is not the best of it...

3. He will dwell with them

One of my best childhood memories is packing into our family car twice a year for the 12-hour journey to visit our grandparents. For a five-year-old boy, every bit of these trips was thrilling—the midnight start, the 3am gas-station pitstop, the greasy fast-food breakfast. The closer we got, the more excited my brothers and I became.

I have to admit that much of our excitement was fueled by my grandmother's tendency to dish out chocolate pretty freely, and by the presence of a ping-pong table, a big television, and a nearby swimming pool. There were also the mini-golf outings and dinners at restaurants. And did I mention the chocolate?

But these perks weren't what got us most excited. When we pulled up outside the house and bolted from our car, we didn't run for the chocolate or the television. We ran for Grandma and Grandpa. Seeing them was what we loved most, and their presence somehow increased our pleasure in all the other good things. If they hadn't been there, the ping-pong and pool and even the chocolate wouldn't have been anywhere near as enjoyable. Arriving at their empty house would have been disappointing rather than delightful.

I hope that the last chapter left you optimistic and excited about the future of this world. The kind of world we all yearn for deep down is the world we all can have. But we haven't yet focused on the main delight, the one that animates all the others. If we stopped after Chapter Two, our anticipation of the new creation would be bizarrely incomplete, like yearning for a trip to the seashore while forgetting the sea, or longing for a meal while ignoring the food.

The central joy of the new creation is not God's gifts; it is God himself. Yes, of course we'll enjoy all the good things, but mostly we'll enjoy the One who actually makes those good things good. God's presence is what puts the newness in new creation, the perfection in perfect life.

That's why the presence of God is central in the two passages we've been focusing on:

> God's dwelling-place is now among the people, and he will dwell with them. They will be his people, and God himself will be with them and be their God. "He will wipe every tear from their eyes." (Revelation 21 v 3-4)

> The throne of God and of the Lamb will be in the city, and his servants will serve him. They will see his face, and his name will be on their foreheads. There will be no more night. They will not need the light of a lamp or the light of the sun, for the Lord God will give them light. (22 v 3-5)

This is a report from another world—it cannot possibly come from this one. No one in history (with the exception of a certain first-century Jewish carpenter) has ever known God like this. To taste this much of God you must travel to a new world—to the new creation, where God is present and God is love.

God is present

When the loud voice from the throne proclaims: "God's dwelling-place is now among the people, and he will dwell with them" (21 v 3), it twice uses an unusual word. That verse says, literally: "Now the tabernacle of God is with men, and he will tabernacle with them." What does that mean?

In the Old Testament, the tabernacle was a portable tent which moved with Israel during their journey through the wilderness. And it was God's temporary solution to a problem as old as humankind. When Adam and Eve sinned in the Garden of Eden, they were exiled from the garden and prevented from returning by an angel and a flaming sword. Outside the garden, life became difficult and painful. But by far their greatest loss was intimate fellowship with God. Separation from God is a terrible thing. Total separation from God is the ultimate curse, the blackest nightmare, a life without any hope or pleasure or joy. By sinning, Adam and Eve took a big step away from God. You could say that all the rest of history is the unfolding of God's plan to bring people back into his presence.

In a couple of ways, Israel's tabernacle provided a solution for sinful people who longed to dwell with God. First, it was the place of sacrifice, where animals were killed and offered to God, and where Israel could seek forgiveness from him. Second, it allowed a pure, holy God to live among his sinful people because it kept God separate from his people. In both the tabernacle and its eventual replacement, the temple, God's presence was focused in a central section of the tabernacle, the "Most Holy Place." The people were never allowed to enter this holiest place. If they tried, they would die (Exodus 33 v 20). Only the high priest entered the Most Holy Place, only once a year, and then only for a few minutes and only after elaborate preparations.

Because God was separated from his people by the tabernacle, he could be present among his people in the tabernacle.

Because God was there, the tabernacle was a place of blessing and delight, a place for feasting and celebrating and worshiping with family and friends (Deuteronomy 12 v 17-18). For ancient Israelites meat was a luxury, rather than the result of a quick trip to McDonalds. Yet when they came to the tabernacle, they could feast on portions of the meat they sacrificed. So, the tabernacle was like your favorite steak restaurant and your beloved church deciding to do a merger. When we think "tabernacle," we should think: "PARTY!" And God was the center of the party. You wanted to be at the tabernacle because that's where God was (read Psalm 63 v 1-2 and see for yourself).

Back now to the voice from the throne in Revelation 21: "Now the tabernacle of God is with men, and he will tabernacle with them." In the new creation, God will come near to his people. In this life we sometimes feel close to God, but sometimes we can't feel him at all. When God tabernacles with us, we'll live in full, intimate, constant knowledge of him. We won't worry, because we'll always feel his care. We won't be insecure, because we'll always know his love. We won't sin, because we won't want to—we'll be totally content in our life with God. When God tabernacles with us, there will be forgiveness, joy, feasting, and worship.

But John's vision gets more amazing still... God doesn't just pitch his tent and invite us to camp alongside him. No, he opens his tent flap and beckons us to come inside, forever.

I've been in some one-of-a-kind rooms, including the Jungle Room in Elvis Presley's mansion, Graceland, in Memphis, Tennessee. Its floors and ceiling are covered with green shag carpet—good for recording music, but as ugly as it sounds! It's a strange, unique place. No room, though, has ever been more distinctive than the Most Holy Place, the place of God's perfect presence in the tabernacle. It looked unlike any other room in the Bible or in Israel's history. It was in the shape of a perfect cube, and overlaid with pure gold (1 Kings 6 v 20). It was the only place like it. Large golden cube = Most Holy Place, the place of God's full, pure presence.

So, what John sees in his vision is shocking:

> [The angel] measured the city with the rod and found it to
> be ... as wide and high as it is long ... The wall was made of
> jasper, and the city of pure gold, as pure as glass.
>
> (Revelation 21 v 16, 18)

Here's a golden cube, here's the place of God's presence, and it's... well... it's an entire city, the eternal "New Jerusalem." In other words, what John sees is God's people living forever in the Most Holy Place. Unthinkable! Israel could visit the tabernacle, but of course they would never have dreamed of entering the golden cube, let alone moving all their possessions into it and settling down to live there. But every citizen of the new creation will enjoy at all times an intimacy with God that only the Jewish high priest got once a year. We'll live in the Most Holy Place. How's that for a street address?! I'm looking forward to the upgrade. We're moving into God's house!

And so God's people will "see his face" (22 v 4). There will be nothing between us and God. He won't withhold himself from us in any way. We'll have as much of his presence as we're able to receive. We'll have unequaled depth of communication and understanding:

> Now we see only a reflection as in a mirror; then we shall see
> face to face. Now I know in part; then I shall know fully, even
> as I am fully known. (1 Corinthians 13 v 12)

We know a person best by seeing their face. I can confirm that this is true from my relationship with my wife, Emma. When I leave my dirty clothes on top of the laundry basket for the umpteenth time (instead of inside, where they belong), a quick glance at Emma's face alerts me to my mistake. Studying her elbow or knee does not yield this important knowledge. More positively, I can communicate affection and sympathy and tenderness toward Emma by looking into her eyes and speaking with her face to face. It's just not the same if I address myself to her foot or ankle. My efforts seem to be largely squandered in such cases.

Does a face-to-face future with God sound good to you? If you're a Christian, it surely does. God doesn't just give us a future, he is our future.

God is love

God's presence with us forever is the best possible news, but only because he will show us love forever. If he was angry with us, closeness to him would be a curse, not a blessing. It would mean destruction, not life. Let's not miss the intimacy and belonging in the last chapters of the Bible:

> They will be his people, and God himself will be with them and be their God. "He will wipe every tear from their eyes."
>
> (Revelation 21 v 3-4)

> The throne of God and of the Lamb will be in the city, and his servants will serve him. They will see his face, and his name will be on their foreheads. There will be no more night. They will not need the light of a lamp or the light of the sun, for the Lord God will give them light.　(22 v 3-5)

We'll be identified by God's name on our foreheads. It couldn't be any clearer that God takes us publicly and joyfully as "his people." We belong to him.

But even more amazingly, God belongs to us: "God himself will ... be their God." In a sense, we are defined by our relationships, for better or worse. I am my parents' son, my wife's husband, my children's father, my church's pastor. What they do and say reflects on me. Who they are is part of who I am. And in an act of breathtaking love, God identifies himself by his relationship with us—he is our God, and we are his people. His love and care and compassion and generosity will be seen in how he cares for us.

Some people are afraid heaven will be a boring place, as though maybe after a few thousand years we'll be like the kid who asks his mother: "What can I do now?" But because the new creation is mainly about knowing God, that will never happen. We'll always be experiencing new facets of God's love for us, and growing in our knowledge of who God is. As the final verse of the hymn *Amazing Grace* says:

> When we've been there ten thousand years,
> Bright shining as the sun,
> We've no less days to sing God's praise
> Than when we've first begun.

In eternity, we won't run out of days. Just as importantly, we won't run out of praise! After ten thousand years, we'll still be discovering new things to praise God for. Our songs will never end.

But isn't God with us now?

The promise of God's presence with his people in the new creation raises a question: isn't he present with us now?

Yes, and no. God the Son, Jesus, told his disciples before he left them to return to heaven: "I am with you always, to the very end of the age" (Matthew 28 v 20). It's not the end of the age yet, so we are included in that promise. And yet Jesus also told those same disciples that he would be "taken away" from them (Matthew 9 v 15).

So is Jesus present, or absent?! The answer is: both, at the same time. He's present with us now, but by his Spirit rather than in a body. And our experience of him is marred by our sin, apathy, and ignorance. In the new creation, Jesus will be fully present with us, and our sin and weakness will no longer diminish our experience of him.

A friend of mine once lived far from his future wife for a year while they were dating. Because they were living in different countries, communication was limited to letters and one weekly phone call. The phone call was the highlight of his week, because it made his girlfriend present. But talking on the phone didn't replace being with her in person—it made him long to be with her even more. It produced a joy and an ache in his heart.

Now imagine that one day, as my friend was speaking to his girlfriend on the phone, he'd heard a knock on the door and opened it to see her standing there, laughing at his surprise. Would he have continued the phone conversation? No way. He'd have dropped the phone, embraced her, and spoken face to face.

Our current experience of God is like that. What we know of God's presence doesn't make us want his full presence less, but more. Our taste increases hunger. Hearing his voice makes us want to see his face. The more we know God now, the more excited we get about the day we will know him completely.

A big question

God tells us that a day is coming when we'll enter his tent. But we're not there yet. We live for now with a kind of "present absence" a partial experience of the full reality. If we want more, that's good! We're meant to want more.

It's worth checking that we're excited about the new creation; and then checking that what we're most excited about is God. If you had asked me on one of those early childhood trips to visit my grandparents why I was so excited, I would have said: "Because I get to see Grandma and Grandpa!" Ah, but what about the pool and the candy? Have you forgotten the television? To those questions, I would have said: "Well, yeah, of course those too. Definitely those! But they're so much better because they come with my grandparents."

The best thing about the new creation is God. So here's a question that challenges me, yet also inspires me, that John Piper poses in *God is the Gospel*: "If you could have heaven, with no sickness, and with all the friends you ever had on earth, and all the food you ever liked, and all the leisure activities you ever enjoyed, and all the natural beauties you ever saw, all the physical pleasures you ever tasted, and no human conflict or any natural disasters, could you be satisfied with heaven, if Christ were not there?"

The new creation is full of great things. If you are sick or in pain, of course you are looking forward to having a perfect body. If you are grieving for a loved one who died a Christian, of course you are looking forward to seeing them again. But these things, wonderful as they are, are not the best thing about your future. You are going to live with God. You are going to enjoy your perfect body with God. You are going to experience a reunion which God attends. He is what makes the perfect future perfect.

But—and this is a big but—*will it really happen?* The world John has pictured for us is a wonderful, perfect place, and it's good to be able to imagine such a future—but will this world really, truly get there? And will you?

4. The future is certain

When I was a little kid, my father used to play an odd game with my brothers and me. He would begin innocently enough: "Boys, would you like a big bowl of ice cream?" Of course we did. "OK. Would you like some hot fudge poured all over it?" Yes, yes! "Great. How about some sprinkles and a cherry on top?!" By now, our excitement was at fever pitch. We knew what was coming and could hardly wait. "Soooooorrrrry, we don't have any!"

For some bizarre reason, this always generated howls of laughter. My family may sound kind of weird. I've tried the game on my own kids, and they laugh as hysterically as I used to. Chalk it up to a genetic flaw.

The first two chapters of this book have described the best bowl of ice cream you will ever eat. But it doesn't matter how good it tastes if "we don't have any!" For the Bible's thrilling descriptions of the new creation to be good news, they must be true news. It's not enough for God to announce an amazing future; he must also secure it. Who wants a golden future of fool's gold? It's worthless.

Actually, it's worse than worthless. It is devastating. That's because human beings eat, drink, and breathe hope. We live and lean toward the future. Advertisers exploit this all the time. If we'll just ride, read, play with, listen to, watch or wear the product they're selling, we'll become the person we've always hoped to be. Our hard-wired future focus means that the ultimate future we've considered in Chapters Two and Three of this book matters. It will change how we live now—and that means that if it will never actually happen, we're wasting our time living toward it. Why would you give up anything now for something that won't happen later? If God will really transform this world into a perfect place and let me live there with him forever, then I'm willing to give up some things now to live for then. But if he can't guarantee this future, I think I'll just cut in line, have my say, stand up for my rights, and take the last piece of pie.

We may not think of it this way, but the big question that shapes our here and now is: will God deliver on the new creation there and then?

He will because he has

The Bible does not give us the answer we might expect it to. It does not say: *Yes, God will deliver.* Instead, we find something much more radical: *God has already delivered.*

Or, to say it another way, God will win because God has won. Evil will be defeated because evil has been defeated. The future is not up for grabs. God has already seized and secured it. The future has already started.

If this sounds a bit mystifying, hang in there. It's well worth taking time to understand. The best way to see it is to consider one of the most strange, surprising and wonderful things Jesus ever said:

> If I drive out demons by the finger of God, then the kingdom
> of God has come upon you. (Luke 11 v 20)

When he spoke these words, Jesus—God's all-powerful, Spirit-filled Son—had just driven out a demon. He was not making an academic, theoretical point: he was explaining what was happening. The kingdom of God had come.

If this sounds neither strange nor surprising nor wonderful to us, it's because we're not hearing it the way the people of Jesus' day would have. We need to back up for a moment and then return to Jesus' words armed with an understanding of three important concepts. So, here we go: a crash course in Old Testament theology!

The kingdom of God

We'll begin with the kingdom of God. In the Old Testament era, God's people held together two truths. First, God was the great King of the whole world: "the LORD is enthroned as King forever" (Psalm 29 v 10). Second, God wasn't exerting the full force of his kingly rule. His kingdom had not yet fully come.

Naturally, the desire of God's suffering people was for their King to assert his reign fully. They knew when he did, there would be judgment for his enemies and salvation for his people:

> In that day the LORD will punish the powers in the heavens
> above and the kings on the earth below. They will be herded
> together like prisoners bound in a dungeon; they will be shut
> up in prison and be punished after many days. The moon
> will be dismayed, the sun ashamed; for the LORD Almighty
> will reign on Mount Zion and in Jerusalem, and before its
> elders—with great glory. (Isaiah 24 v 21-23)

"The LORD Almighty will reign" in a way that he was not yet reigning as Isaiah spoke. None of his enemies would be a match for his power. And the glory of his kingdom would shine so brightly that the sun and moon would feel ashamed of their paltry light! The coming of the kingdom is like a fireworks display: big, public, and climactic. No one will miss it. The glory of God will destroy his enemies and delight his people.

This age, and the age to come

But when will this kingdom of justice and glory come? Jesus, and the New Testament authors, saw history as divided into two ages. The first was "this age," marked by sin, suffering and death. The second was "the age to come," when the kingdom would arrive. Here are a couple of brief examples:

> Anyone who speaks against the Holy Spirit will not be
> forgiven, either in this age or in the age to come.
>
> (Matthew 12 v 32)

> Grace and peace to you from God our Father and the Lord
> Jesus Christ, who gave himself for our sins to rescue us from
> the present evil age. (Galatians 1 v 3-4)

The day of the LORD

The final concept to grasp in order to understand Jesus' teaching about the kingdom of God is the day of the LORD; the climactic day separating this age from the age to come. It's there in the Isaiah passage we saw above: "In that day the LORD will punish the powers in the heavens above and the kings on the earth below." Isaiah warned that the day of the LORD would be a terrible day for God's enemies, because the kingdom had come:

> Wail, for the day of the LORD is near; it will come like
> destruction from the Almighty. Because of this, all hands will
> go limp, every heart will melt with fear.   (Isaiah 13 v 6-7)

But again, there's a flip side. The day of the LORD is cause for celebration among God's people—because it is the day the kingdom will come:

> In that day the LORD Almighty will be a glorious crown, a
> beautiful wreath for the remnant of his people. (28 v 5)

The present age will not fade gently and imperceptibly into the age to come. There will be an abrupt, dramatic, public and climactic transition. There will be fireworks.

Jesus' radical claim

Now we're in a good position to understand what Jesus is saying about the kingdom of God. Jesus had just thrown a demon out of a man, and some in the gathered crowd accused him of driving out demons by the power of Satan (Luke 11 v 15). In mounting his defense against this charge, Jesus argued it would be nonsensical for Satan to work against himself. And he clarified where his ability to cast out demons actually came from:

> But if I drive out demons by the finger of God, then the
> kingdom of God has come upon you. When a strong man,
> fully armed, guards his own house, his possessions are safe.
> But when someone stronger attacks and overpowers him, he
> takes away the armor in which the man trusted and divides
> up his plunder. (v 20-22)

The coming of the kingdom of God means battle. Jesus is attacking and overpowering Satan, the "strong man" who has now met his match. The visible display of this spiritual conflict is the exorcisms. They reveal that God has asserted his reign and brought his kingdom.

The rest of Luke's Gospel and the New Testament as a whole make clear that Satan's defeat occurs ultimately through Jesus' death and resurrection. Paul says that at the cross, God:

> disarmed the rulers and authorities and put them to open shame, by triumphing over them in [Jesus].
>
> (Colossians 2 v 15, ESV)

So, when Jesus says "the kingdom has come," he means it comes through his life and ministry as a whole (including the cross and resurrection). Notice Jesus doesn't say the kingdom "will" come. The verb is past tense. It has come.

But this claim must have sounded seriously bizarre to the people listening to him. Remember, the kingdom of God comes with a fireworks display of judgment and glory. It made no sense for Jesus to say—while life apparently continued on as it always had—that the kingdom had already come.

Those around Jesus knew their Bibles. They were waiting for God's kingdom, the start of the age to come, beginning with God's victory on the day of the Lord at the end of history. But now Jesus was saying that God's victory comes in the midst of history. God's victory is initially going to look more like a few firecrackers than a fireworks extravaganza.

Jesus knew how scandalous this teaching was. But he didn't back down from it. Instead, he pressed in on this exact point with two parables. He wanted to show how small, hidden, and unimpressive God's kingdom looked as it arrived through him:

> "What is the kingdom of God like? What shall I compare it to? It is like a mustard seed, which a man took and planted in

his garden. It grew and became a tree, and the birds perched in its branches." Again he asked, "What shall I compare the kingdom of God to? It is like yeast that a woman took and mixed into about sixty kilograms of flour until it worked all through the dough."   (Luke 13 v 18-21)

The thing about a seed is, you can't see it. That's why it was such an anticlimax when we planted a garden with our children last year. We built the raised beds (loud pounding of nails is good), we filled them with soil (dirty, therefore fun), we planted the seeds (icky, because we were using manure, but exciting), and then... nothing. The seeds just disappeared into the soil. Nothing at all happened, even after five whole minutes of patient waiting by both children. Boring!

But the seeds did grow. After a while, the garden became a lot more interesting. Our raised beds were eventually overrun with gargantuan, unruly tomato plants. Jesus' parables of the seed and the yeast show that the kingdom of God will eventually come in a big, public, climactic fashion. It will be a full-scale tree. The hidden yeast will be mixed throughout the dough. God's enemies will get the judgment they deserve; God's people the mercy they don't.

When we think of the kingdom as that full-scale tree, it's right to say the kingdom has not yet come. But the seed will become the tree. The seed is as much made of kingdom stuff as the tree is. So in the seed, the kingdom has already come. Nothing can prevent it becoming the tree.

Although God has not exerted his reign finally, he has exerted it decisively. His kingdom is unstoppable because it is already here. God's enemies are defeated—they just don't know it yet. When Jesus came, the kingdom seed was sown. Through Jesus, God has already changed the world forever. And if we understand this truth, it will change us.

Start the celebrations

Suppose your brother is in a world-championship tic-tac-toe tournament (noughts and crosses, for UK readers) and you've bet your house, your car, and all your future earnings on him winning. He's reached the final, but now he's up against last year's world champion, who, scouting reports indicate, is on top form. Will your brother win? He's practiced long and hard; he's sharpened his favorite pencil; but you can't know. Everything you have, your whole future, hangs on this contest; but you can have no confidence he'll win.

The match begins. Here's your brother's opening move:

Then his opponent, bizarrely, places his "O" here:

Pouncing on his unexpected blunder, your brother places an "X" in the upper left hand corner of the board:

Are you confident now? You should be! Your brother has won the game (if you're wondering how you can know your brother's won, see bottom of next page). Your bet has paid off! It's over!

Except that it isn't. The game is won, but it's also not won. His opponent is defeated, but he's also not yet defeated. There is no way your brother will lose now, because of the positions on the grid. But the game still needs to play out to its inevitable conclusion. Victory has been achieved, but not yet fully implemented. The champagne isn't yet flowing, but you are already celebrating.

The announcement of the New Testament—the message of the gospel—is that Jesus has won, and Jesus will win. The latter follows surely from the former. We can live with total certainty about where the world is heading, because of what Jesus has already accomplished through his life, death, and resurrection. We can live with the confidence of living between the third tic-tac-toe board above, and the end of the game.

In Chapters Two and Three of this book, we were actually glimpsing the full and final coming of God's kingdom. That's what the new creation is. John himself says it this way:

> The kingdom of the world has become the kingdom of our
> Lord and of his Messiah, and he will reign forever and ever.
>
> (Revelation 11 v 15)

How do we know—really know, not just wish or guess—that God will make good on this future and bring his completed kingdom? Because of Jesus' astounding words: "The kingdom of God has come upon you." He's already done it. It's already here. The enemy is already defeated. The seed will become the giant tree. God will finish what he's begun.

If you want to be completely confident that the world is heading for perfection, look no further than Jesus—his life, death and resurrection. That's where we get certainty that the kingdom has come, and that nothing will stop this world reaching the flawless future God has planned for it.

And, as we saw in the first two chapters, there'll be people living in that world. Oh, to be one of them! But... what if I'm not? What if you're not? After all, this could all be true, every

---

Here's why you can be so confident your brother has won the game: his opponent will have to place his "O" top middle, and your brother can then place his next "X" bottom left:

Now, wherever his opponent puts his "O", your brother will be able to complete a row of three with his next "X". He's won!

word; but not include us. We might be going the wrong way in life to get there. We might get lost on the way. We might get bounced at the door. How can we know that when we reach the new creation we'll be welcomed in rather than turned away?

5. *Your* future is certain

A group of friends sits around a table in the corner of a restaurant after a funeral. Someone says, as someone always does at these times: "Well, at least he's in a better place." In the silence that follows, each person's thoughts turn to themselves.

Frank is the one who made the comment. He's a spiritual person. He believes God is love. That means everyone will enjoy a happy future. God wouldn't want anyone to suffer. Frank finds that knowledge really comforting at this time.

Next to Frank sits Ben. He's a Christian, but right now that's not comforting him. He's really struggling in his faith; yesterday he blew it again and gave in to temptation. Thoughts of death and the "better place" fill him with a sinking feeling. He keeps messing up; he has serious doubts at times. Is he really going there? Is he going to last?

Amy's feeling much better. "I'm a Christian," she thinks. "I'll be fine. I'm glad I can sit here knowing that—glad that I've never done anything really bad, and that I know how to live God's way and go to church, so that he'll let me in."

Sarah, on the other hand, is feeling anything but fine. She's never thought much about God, death or the afterlife. She's thinking about it today, though. Is there a better place, and is

Jesus part of it? And if he is, Jesus wouldn't want someone like her there anyway... would he? Is there anything she could do to be welcomed there?

Julie is a humble, hopeful Christian. The funeral has reminded her of how much she's looking forward to being in God's new creation, and she's so grateful to Jesus for what he's done to give her that hope. The thought of not being there doesn't cross her mind, any more than the thought of not going home after the meal does.

There's a great deal of confidence, and a great deal of anxiety, around that table. There's a variety of views about how you get to a "better place." I wonder if you hear any of your own private hopes, concerns and struggles reflected in these thoughts? Reading this chapter would challenge some of the people around that table about their confidence; it would encourage some to leave their worries behind; it would excite some, and likely offend others. Truth does that.

Confident?

Imagine you're a member of a professional baseball team (maybe this is as much of a stretch for you as it is for me, but use your imagination!). Your team has just clinched a place in the post-season playoffs. You join the locker-room celebration; but you join in halfheartedly. Why? Because your performance on the field has been lousy recently, and you have a strong suspicion you won't be allowed to stay on the team. You're confident the team is going on to glory; but you fear you may just be going home.

You get the point. A full celebration of God's future is reserved for those who know it's their future. When we're confident we'll be there, the joy of the new creation breaks into our present. As the seventeenth-century Puritan preacher Thomas Brooks said, having assurance of salvation is like living in the suburbs of paradise. It's the next best thing to actually being there.

But we can't make ourselves part of the future of this world simply by saying so. It is, after all, God's future. We have to let him tell us how to get there. When we hear and receive his surprising words about who makes it to the new creation and how, we can avoid false assurance and enjoy godly confidence.

Let's look to Jesus' teaching in John 5 in order to discover the relationship between God's future and ours. Jesus' words speak directly to Frank, Ben, Amy, Sarah, and Julie... and also to us.

> I tell you, whoever hears my word and believes him who sent me has eternal life and will not be judged but has crossed over from death to life. Very truly I tell you, a time is coming and has now come when the dead will hear the voice of the Son of God and those who hear will live. For as the Father has life in himself, so he has granted the Son also to have life in himself. And he has given him authority to judge because he is the Son of Man. Do not be amazed at this, for a time is coming when all who are in their graves will hear his voice and come out—those who have done what is good will rise to live, and those who have done what is evil will rise to be condemned. (John 5 v 24-29)

Life, life, and life

Jesus' teaching is exciting, but it requires unraveling. The key is to realize that Jesus uses the word "life" in three different ways.

First, there's biological life, the life we're living now. When Jesus heals someone, it's this type of life he restores. Biological life is a precious gift; but it's of limited value. It guarantees no relationship with God—many people are physically alive, but spiritually dead.

And it's temporary—everyone who is born into this life leaves this life.

Second, there's resurrection life. It's far superior to biological life, because it lasts forever. It's a life Jesus promises:

> A time is coming when all who are in their graves will hear his voice and come out—those who have done what is good will rise to live, and those who have done what is evil will rise to be condemned. (v 28-29)

For some, there is a life coming that is a perfect existence in the perfect new creation—this is resurrection life. But there's a problem with it. Jesus says that "a time is coming." That means it's not here yet. Resurrection life is great, but it's all in the future. And it's not in the future for everyone—some will rise to perfect life in perfect bodies, but others will find themselves condemned to enduring existence without anything good.

So we come to the third sense of "life," which falls between biological life and resurrection life. Like biological life, this kind of life is something we can experience now, not just in the future. And like resurrection life, it lasts forever, rather than being merely temporary. This life is both now and forever. Like biological life and resurrection life, it comes by hearing Jesus' voice:

> Whoever hears my word and believes him who sent me has eternal life and will not be judged but has crossed over from death to life. Very truly I tell you, a time is coming and has now come when the dead will hear the voice of the Son of God and those who hear will live. (v 24-25)

This is a life which "has now come." We can begin it now. Jesus called it "eternal life" (17 v 3). Eternal life means living in relationship with God through Jesus Christ. It's about quantity (how long life lasts) and quality (how good life is).

So, what does Jesus' teaching have to do with the hopes and fears of Frank, Ben, Amy, Sarah, and Julie?

Jesus achieves eternal life

Jesus says we may have eternal life now, rather than being condemned by God at the last day, just by hearing and believing (5 v 24). Is that all that has to happen for us to have eternal life? Yes, and no. Yes, in that it is all we need to do. But the reason that this is all we have to do is because Jesus has done everything else needed.

You may well have heard many times, in a variety of ways, what Jesus has done to offer eternal life. But I want to take us now a couple of chapters earlier in John, to what is perhaps a less well-known explanation from the lips of Jesus; one in which, surprisingly, he compares himself to a snake:

> Just as Moses lifted up the snake in the wilderness, so the
> Son of Man must be lifted up, that everyone who believes
> may have eternal life in him. (3 v 14-15)

Christ is recalling an episode from centuries before, in the long years the nation of Israel spent wandering through the wilderness, on their way from captivity in Egypt to their new home in Canaan.

Israel was griping about the manna God had provided, calling it "miserable food" (Numbers 21 v 5). God's response was to send venomous snakes to kill the complainers.

That may sound like an overreaction, but it wasn't. By this time, Israel had been freed from Egypt by God, had had food provided by God, and had been given success in battle by God. Yet instead of thanking him and trusting him, they were grumbling about his plans and provision. In complaining about the manna, they were rejecting God, not just his menu.

Israel was basically saying to God: *We don't want life on your terms, in relationship with you, in your world.* God was saying to Israel: *Then I will take that life away.* Venomous snakes were a normal part of desert life; miraculous food was not. God's judgment was to give Israel what they wanted; life, and therefore death, without him. Sending all those snakes was God's fitting response to Israel's attitude.

But they were not his last word. He offered his people a way out of the judgment he had brought on them. He told Moses to make a bronze snake and lift it on a pole. Having been bitten, knowing they would die, if they looked at the bronze snake on the pole, they would live. They could do nothing to save themselves; but they didn't need to.

It is a strange episode, not because of the judgment that came, but because of the means of salvation that followed. A bronze snake, lifted high on a pole, gave life.

And that snake was a picture of a greater rescue:

> Just as Moses lifted up the snake in the wilderness, so the
> Son of Man must be lifted up. (John 3 v 14)

Like the Israelites, all people in this world have rebelled against God and stand under his judgment. We've chosen to live without him, so we will die without him, and face eternity without him and anything good. And we can do nothing to save ourselves. We've been bitten by death; it's coming. We're goners.

But, like the bronze snake, Jesus was "lifted up," on a cross. Though as "the Son of Man" he had come from heaven (v 13), though he never complained or grumbled or disobeyed his Father, though he deserved eternal life, he died. He bore God's judgment. He took the venom of death and hell that we deserve, so that he can share with us the life he deserves.

There is only one way to avoid eternal death and enjoy eternal life: believe. "Everyone who believes may have [ie: will have] eternal life" (v 15). I must look to Jesus. I must see in Jesus' life and death my only opportunity to escape death and have life.

How does this play around the table in that restaurant? It challenges Frank. He thinks everyone is fine with God; but that's as dangerous as a snake-bitten Israelite convincing himself that he and his friends are not dying. And it challenges Amy. She thinks her goodness, church-going and self-identification as a Christian outweigh any sins she may commit, and mean she has eternal life. That's as mistaken as a snake-bitten Israelite ignoring her swollen legs because her arms are fine, and never even wondering why Moses is holding a bronze snake up high.

The truth is, the only way for us to live was for Jesus to die.

Faith receives eternal life

Jesus' death achieves eternal life. But what about Sarah's questions? Would Jesus want her in the new creation? And how would she get this eternal life?

The cross shouts the answer to Sarah's first question: *Yes!* The cross tells her that she is, as she suspects, not able to deserve a place in the new creation; she is a sinner. But the cross also shows her that Jesus still died for her, still offers her the life she shouldn't have. What does she need to do?

> Very truly I tell you, whoever hears my word and believes
> him who sent me has eternal life and will not be judged but
> has crossed from death to life. (5 v 24)

Believe. Have faith. Faith means looking to the cross as the Israelites did to the bronze snake; knowing that this is God's way, and the only way, to be saved. The dying Israelite couldn't treat his own wounds and look at the bronze snake at the same time. He had to choose. Faith is laying down the first-aid kit and looking to the snake. Faith is knowing that without Christ we are hopeless, but that Christ gives certain hope.

But is eternal life really received through faith alone? Jesus says those who have "done evil" rise from their graves to condemnation, while those who have "done good" rise to live forever (v 29). Again, we need to read the Bible in light of the whole Bible. What is the "work" God requires of us? "To believe in the one he has sent" (6 v 29). Everything else—all the "good" we do that pleases God—flows out of first putting our faith for our life and our future in Jesus. It's the evidence of our faith.

This truth honors God and humbles us. The only people who will be welcomed into the new creation are those who know they don't deserve to be there. Julie has it right. Her confidence is grounded in a humble trust in Jesus.

Eternal life guarantees resurrection life (because it is resurrection life)

What about Ben? Ben can be deeply encouraged by understanding two truths. First, by trusting in Jesus he has already received eternal life. Jesus says the one who hears his word and believes "has" (present tense) eternal life. He "has crossed over from death to life." Eternal life is now. Because he believes, Ben has it.

Second, having eternal life in the present guarantees resurrection life in the future. Why? Because eternal life is resurrection life... in seed form. Eternal life and resurrection life aren't so much two different kinds of life as they are two stages in the one gift of unending life with God. The first stage comes now: even as we live in dying bodies, we have living souls. The second stage follows: when Jesus returns, we will be granted resurrection bodies to match our living souls. Jesus connected these two stages inseparably: "For my Father's will is that everyone who looks to the Son and believes in him shall have eternal life, and I will raise them up at the last day" (John 6 v 40). Eternal life is what resurrection life looks like now. It's the acorn that holds the oak tree. To have the acorn is to have the oak (eventually), because the tree is in the seed.

When Ben asks: "How can I know I'll live forever?" the best answer is: "Because you've already begun." Eternal life is not something Ben might get to one day. It's something he's living today. And when Ben asks: "How do I know I've already begun?" the best answer is: "Because you are looking to Jesus, God's Son, for rescue." Eternal life is not something Ben will ever deserve, nor is it something he will ever need to deserve. It's a free gift from Jesus, and it's already his.

A certain future

A few years ago, I had to take the GRE, a major exam required by some graduate schools to which I was applying. I studied for months and then one day drove, white-knuckled, to the testing center. Because I was taking the exam on a computer, I could see my preliminary score as soon as I completed it, though I would have to wait for the official result to arrive in the mail weeks later. After finishing, I swallowed hard and viewed my score...

... and it was far higher than I'd even dared hope! You know how I responded? I didn't say: "This score isn't official or public. I wonder how I'll do?" I began rejoicing! I drove home giddy with excitement, called my family, and celebrated. True, the score wasn't official (it had to be confirmed), or public (it had to be sent to the grad schools). But I already had the score, and I was already celebrating.

Do you know you're going to the new creation? If you know Jesus and know that his death is the source of your life, you have life. You don't need to be anxious, to feel a faint terror at funerals, to lie awake wondering if you'll make it. You don't need to wonder what Jesus will say when you stand before him at the last day. He's already said it. Your eternal life has begun. You'll still sometimes stumble and sin. But your future is certain.

Of course, there is another type of certainty about the future. If we haven't looked to Jesus, the venom is still at work. If we haven't passed from death to life, we're still facing eternal death. You may be reading this book and have realized you're like Amy. You're a good person. You don't do anything really bad. Maybe you go to church, a lot. Perhaps you're even a pastor, or a pastor's spouse. But you've never realized your goodness is hopeless when it comes to gaining eternal life; you've never put your faith in Jesus. You can be certain about what road you are on, and it is not to the new creation. But you can be equally certain that all you need do is stop trusting yourself, and start trusting Jesus, and you will pass from death to life, from heading for hell to heading for the new creation.

If we have heard and believed Jesus' words, our future is wonderful *and* utterly, totally certain. Knowing Jesus makes all the difference for our future; and knowing our future makes all the difference for our present. How? That's what the rest of this book is about.

6. Tightrope walking

In early 2004, I met a young lady named Emma Hutchinson and promptly fell in love with her. I knew within a couple weeks that this was the girl I wanted to marry and grow old with.

There was just one problem: she was nowhere near so sure! Thankfully, my dogged persistence paid off, and we eventually started dating. As time went on, I became more and more sure that Emma would be an amazing wife—but not nearly so sure that she would actually ever *be* my wife. So, when, 18 months after we met, I got down on two knees to propose to Emma (yes, I know it's supposed to be one knee, but I was really nervous) and she said yes, my world changed. We weren't married yet, but now—at last!—I knew that we would be.

I noticed two things about myself in the weeks after our engagement. First, seeing Emma wearing her engagement ring made me less satisfied with my single life. I was no longer blissfully content eating large quantities of microwave meals while watching movies by myself. My personal hygiene began to improve markedly. All my plans for the coming year now included another person. I looked for housing for two, not for one; I drew up a budget for two, not one. I was looking forward to marriage, leaning toward it, planning for it... because I was confident I would soon be married. My future kept pressing into my present. Though I wasn't yet a married man, I was beginning to live like one.

But, oddly enough, at the very same time I was patient. Because I knew Emma would say "I do" at our wedding, I didn't feel the need constantly to check she still loved me and would go through with the marriage. I never considered pushing the wedding to an earlier date before she could change her mind. When I experienced sexual temptation, I would fight it by reminding myself that very soon we would be married: "I don't need this. I can wait."

Confidence about my married future was simultaneously creating restlessness and patience in my present.

The Christian's confidence about their future—that it is wonderful, and that it is certain—has exactly the same paradoxical effect. It produces two impulses within us that we might think wouldn't fit together—it makes us restless and patient for the new creation at the very same time. This is what Paul is explaining in Romans 8:

> We ourselves, who have the firstfruits of the Spirit, groan inwardly as we wait eagerly for our adoption to sonship, the redemption of our bodies. For in this hope we were saved. But hope that is seen is no hope at all. Who hopes for what they already have? But if we hope for what we do not yet have, we wait for it patiently. (8 v 23-25)

Paul refers to future-oriented Christian confidence as "hope": "For in this hope we were saved." We often use the word hope to mean "wish." When hope = wish, hope becomes a very flimsy word, because very often we don't get what we wish for. "I hope they don't serve mushrooms... but they have." "I hope they don't see the mushrooms I've hidden in my napkin... but they have." The Bible sees "hope" very differently; it is not flimsy, but certain.

It is rooted in God's character even though it stretches toward something that hasn't yet happened.

Think of a skyscraper with massive foundations in the ground, soaring light and airy toward the sky. That's biblical hope—an assured confidence of something yet future. Here, the focus of this hope is our full and final welcome into the new creation as God's children, and our enjoyment of renewed bodies. In other words, it's the cast-iron confidence that God will recreate the whole world and will get us there to enjoy it: a new me in a new world. That's Christian hope!

And Paul identifies the twin results of that hope in the verses on either side.

First, Christians "groan inwardly as we wait eagerly for our adoption to sonship, the redemption of our bodies" (v 23). Have you ever wanted something so much (a cold drink on a hot day, a hot shower on a cold day, something sweet during a diet) that you actually groaned for it? Groaning for something means you really, really want it. So, that inward groaning and eager waiting is restlessness. We're not satisfied with this imperfect present, precisely because we're certain of a perfect future.

Second, the strong confidence of a Christian also produces patience: "But if we hope for what we do not yet have, we wait for it patiently" (v 25). We know that we don't have the life we long for; but we also know that we will one day. We don't need to rush it. We don't want to turn away from it. That's patience.

Walking the wire

On June 15, 2012, millions of television viewers around the world watched Nik Wallenda attempt to walk an 1800-foot tightrope across the widest part of Niagara Falls. No one else had ever tried it.

The walk soon became more difficult than Wallenda had expected. Mist from the Falls was so thick that it was hard to see at times. The wind was wild, pummeling him from the front and the back. Because the wire had no supports, it moved in the wind—and it was hard to judge its unpredictable movements because of the turbulent waters rushing past below. Speaking live to television reporters as he moved cautiously forward, he said: "I'm drained. ... My hands are going numb. I feel like I'm getting weak."

The walk was dangerous and exhausting. But it was also delightfully exhilarating. Nik Wallenda was seeing the power and beauty of Niagara Falls from a perspective no one else ever had. The only way to experience it that way was to walk the wire. The hundreds of millions who watched from the safety of solid ground couldn't see what he saw. As he balanced on his wire, looking out over the Falls, he said: "It's a beautiful view; a dream in the making."

The central point of this book is that Christians are meant to live, and can live, in a healthy, exhilarating, joyful, productive, frustrating, painful, challenging tension between restlessness and patience.

It's like walking a tightrope.

The Australian evangelist John Chapman wrote in *A Foot in Two Worlds*: "We must learn to be content with the dissatisfaction of not yet being what we one day will be." He was describing a tightrope! This is the Christian life; walking a tightrope on the way to the new creation. We trust in God's timing (that's patience) even as we ache and yearn for the fulfillment of his promises (that's restlessness).

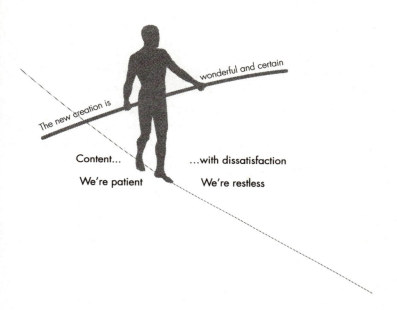

The new creation is wonderful and certain

Content...

We're patient

...with dissatisfaction

We're restless

It's scary to step onto a tightrope. If we tip off either side, it will all go terribly wrong. But take heart; we have help and hope as we edge onto the tightrope of restless patience.

Nik Wallenda had help in his successful crossing of Niagara Falls. He was holding a 40-foot pole for balance. In the next couple of chapters, we'll discover how the dazzling truths we've seen in Chapters Two to Five keep us balanced on the wire of restlessness and patience.

If we're willing to venture onto this wire, it will take us places we couldn't reach by any other means. We'll see and serve the world in new ways. Our walk will be challenging, but also the thrill of a lifetime.

Now, let's get that first foot on the wire...

7. Restlessness

Christians are to "wait eagerly" for the new creation. That means being excited but groaning, positive yet dissatisfied, optimistic while restless.

But hold on. Dissatisfied? Restless? Doesn't the Bible tell us to be content? After all, Paul said:

> I have learned to be content whatever the circumstances. I know what it is to be in need, and I know what it is to have plenty. I have learned the secret of being content in any and every situation, whether well fed or hungry, whether living in plenty or in want. (Philippians 4 v 11-12)

How does restlessness fit with contentment? Do they fit at all? Well, they must—because one of the great Bible passages on restlessness comes just before the contentment passage quoted above. Paul himself saw no contradiction between feeling restless for the future and content in the present... at the same time. Here's how he spoke of his future resurrection life:

> Not that I have ... already arrived at my goal, but I press on to take hold of that for which Christ Jesus took hold of me. Brothers and sisters, I do not consider myself yet to have taken hold of it. But one thing I do: forgetting what is behind and straining toward what is ahead, I press on toward the goal to win the prize for which God has called me heavenward in Christ Jesus. (Philippians 3 v 12-14)

What is going on?!

What restlessness is (and isn't)

Restlessness is a passion for our future in the new creation. Restlessness is aligning our identities, thoughts, actions, and goals with that future. Restlessness is the attitude of not settling for now.

Forgetting what lies behind, Paul is "straining toward" what lies ahead. That phrase is drawn from the Greek athletic games. If you've ever watched a 100-meter sprint, you know the all-out effort and intense forward-focus Paul describes. When a great sprinter comes racing down the track, leaning to dip for the line, he's not thinking about how well he came out of the blocks, or what a great first ten meters he ran. Every fiber is focused forward. Paul says this is the way he lives his life.

In Paul's analogy, the end of the race is the return of Jesus, final salvation, the resurrection of his body. That's what Paul strains forward to reach. It isn't that he never thinks about his past (see 1 Corinthians 15 v 9), but he refuses to rest on past accomplishments or wallow in past defeats. His future in the new creation defines and orients his life. That's what he means by saying he does "one thing." Of course he doesn't stop working, eating, reading, praying, preaching, laughing, and so on. "One thing" means the North Star orienting his present is his future. Paul's daily tasks are undertaken with a view to accomplishing his aim of reaching the finish line.

In other words, Paul didn't settle for now. Paul lived in the present, but he didn't live for the present. He worked hard in the present, but he lived for the future.

This was the secret of Paul's contentment. Biblical restlessness does not undermine contentment. Just the opposite: it undergirds contentment. Because Paul didn't settle for the present, because his eggs weren't in that basket, the present could not control him or determine his inner attitude or well-being. His stomach might be pleasantly full or painfully empty—either way, he was content. That didn't mean he enjoyed the sensation of biting hunger, or that he didn't enjoy the feeling of eating a good meal. But hungry or full, his future in the new creation was secure, and the future is what he was living for. So he could be content. His circumstances neither destroyed nor propped up his contentment.

Living for today, or tomorrow?

This way of life isn't just for Paul—it's for us, too. After all, he says:

> All of us ... who are mature should take such a view of things. And if on some point you think differently, that too God will make clear to you. (v 15)

So... what do we live for? Past, present, or future? What might God make clear to you—even as you read this chapter?

Most of us find it all too easy to live focused on the past. Perhaps we linger on past defeats (mistakes made, wrongs suffered, opportunities missed) and become bitter. Or perhaps we lean on past victories (degrees earned, relationships enjoyed, accomplishments achieved) and become boring.

Or we live for the present. If things are going well at work or home, we feel good about ourselves and happy with the world. If things are going poorly—the sink clogs again, the child throws a tantrum in public again, we fail to meet the sales quota again—we feel bad about ourselves and angry with the world. Either way, we're settling for now, letting it define us, for good or for bad.

This prompts us to ask ourselves some challenging questions.

Here's the first: "Have I settled for now at my job?" Are all my eggs (self-worth, happiness, feelings of success) in the "now" basket? When we forget the future, we may begin to compete in an unhealthy way with co-workers, forgetting that our worth isn't at stake in how well we succeed on the job. If work goes poorly, or if work goes away altogether due to a job loss, forgetters of the future will complain, and eventually despair. If work goes well, we're good... until it goes poorly again.

Christian restlessness as we move through our workday changes the way we work. We look for opportunities to invite co-workers into the eternal joy we'll experience with God. We're content even when work is frustrating, our boss unfair, and our co-workers annoying.

Second challenging question: "Have I settled for now in parenting?" Do we despair that God hasn't given us the perfect kids we'd imagined parenting? Do we despair that God hasn't given us any children at all? If I'm honest, I have to admit that my parenting of my three young children is too often focused exclusively on the present, as I respond in the moment to my children's behavior (whether good or bad). If you plotted my happiness/contentment levels and my children's behavior on the same graph, they'd often correspond very closely!

It's difficult to keep the bigger picture of their eternal future (not just their present behavior) in view. But as the vision of biblical restlessness has gripped me, I've begun to pray differently for my children. In addition to praying for their daily needs and struggles, I now ask God to prepare them to live forever in the new creation. Everything else I do as a parent is to be oriented around that goal.

Third challenging question: you will know what it is. We are all different, with different characters and enjoying or enduring different circumstances. So the temptation to locate our contentment in an aspect of our life right now will look different for all of us; but it will be there. There may well be a question you need to ask yourself, where you complete the sentence: "Have I settled for now in...?"

The tragedy of settling

Now I need to offer a warning.

If you've settled for now, you have placed yourself on a path to inevitable despair. Why? Because we live in a broken, sinful world. God still hasn't fully asserted his kingly rule over the earth. Because it's broken, this world cannot satisfy. The absolute best job won't perfectly satisfy. Nor will the best house, marriage, food, or vacation. Settling for now is the path to despair.

Here's an irony: the best way to enjoy this world is to not settle for it. When you see this world as a preparation for the next, not as the be-all-and-end-all to your happiness, you can suffer its disappointments without being crushed, and savor its delights without forgetting there's better to come.

The writer of Hebrews says a breathtaking thing to his readers:

> You suffered along with those in prison and joyfully accepted
> the confiscation of your property, because you knew that you
> yourselves had better and lasting possessions. (10 v 34)

Do you see what he's saying? Joy in an imperfect present flows to us from a perfect future. If our joy is in the things we have now, losing them is the worst thing that can happen; all our joy goes with them. If, like these Christians, our joy is in the things we will enjoy in our eternal future, nothing we might lose now can touch our joy. We're free to enjoy the things we have now without worrying about their impermanence; we're free to lose them without feeling that our life has gone, too.

Biblical restlessness doesn't mean hating or neglecting the present. It doesn't mean always wishing we were somewhere else. It means seeing now as a preparation for forever, aligning our present with our future. Have you ever stayed overnight in a hotel room on a long trip, and been so impressed with its beauty that you forgot the rest of your trip and decided to live there indefinitely? Of course not. No matter how great the hotel room, it's a temporary stop on the way to your final destination. Now is preparation for forever. Have you ever stayed in a hotel room with dirty carpets, a moldy shower, and cheesy décor? I have (in New Haven—I won't name the hotel, but you know who you are!). Staying in that room wasn't pleasant, but it didn't ruin my month. It wasn't my home—we were there for just a night. And it was getting us closer to our final destination.

Do you find your focus terminating on now? God created you with a future as wide as the new creation—don't shrink it to the size of a Facebook page or a hobby room or a computer game. Don't settle. Stretch forward.

Why aren't we more restless?

So, why aren't we more restless for the new creation? One reason is that we've bought into the massive misconception of our culture that it will be boring. It's become common to imagine heaven as a long worship service, or a place of clouds and harp-playing. One cartoon shows a man with angel wings sitting alone on a cloud, saying: "I wish I'd brought a magazine." In Mark Twain's *The Adventures of Huckleberry Finn*, Huck's response to Miss Watson's description of heaven as a place of harp-playing and singing is:

> I didn't think much of it ... I asked her if she reckoned Tom Sawyer would go there, and she said, not by a considerable sight. I was glad about that, because I wanted him and me to be together.

Of course we don't yearn for that kind of future. Why would we?

There's another reason we're not restless for the new creation: we're not really certain it is our future. Don't get me wrong— if you're a Christian, I'm sure you believe in your mind the Bible's teaching about the new creation. But do you believe it in practice? The way we live reveals what we functionally believe. If you're a Christian and you spend the clear majority of your time dominated with past or present joys, victories, goals, concerns, worries, and fears, then you're not living as if you're actually confident the new creation is where you'll soon be.

If the new creation doesn't sound really good and feel really certain, we won't live restlessly toward it.

How can we be more restless?

The best way to be restless is to be captivated by the future's beauty and convinced that the future is ours. That's why chapters Two to Five came first in this book. We could all do a lot worse than regularly reading John 5 and Revelation 21 – 22! When we grasp that our future is wonderfully with God, and that it is totally certain, our lives will reflect it. As we understand that the kingdom has already come, and that we already have eternal life, we won't settle for now—any more than I was willing to settle for my unshaven, disheveled "now" after getting engaged to my wonderful future wife.

Look where Paul turns his thoughts as he writes about straining forward and contentment in the present:

> Our citizenship is in heaven. And we eagerly await a Savior from there, the Lord Jesus Christ, who, by the power that enables him to bring everything under his control, will transform our lowly bodies so that they will be like his glorious body. (Philippians 3 v 20-21)

Paul thinks about the presence of Christ in heaven and the awesome promise of a glorious resurrection body. His meditation produces eager expectation. There's no substitute for prayerfully meditating upon the world to come. Great Christians throughout history have done this. The Puritan pastor Richard Baxter said that as he grew older, he meditated more frequently upon heaven, and preferred it to any other topic. It's like reading a glossy brochure of a holiday destination we'd love to visit. As we allow the Bible to whet our appetite for the new creation, we grow restless to be there.

Three tips

So, how in practice can we help ourselves see that then is so much better than now?

First, we should stay alert for reminders of the flaws of this present world. Think of the financial crisis of 2008, in which the greed, foolishness and dishonesty of the financial sector was revealed to the world. The financial bubble of the early 2000s looked too good to be true because it *was* too good to be true. Of course, stock markets aren't the only places with false fronts. Hollywood thrives on a veneer of glamour and beauty. But the inner brokenness of even its biggest stars sometimes bubbles over—think drug rehab and marriage breakdowns and embarrassing arrests. These are reminders of the reality behind appearances.

Second, we should allow God to use pain and inconvenience in our lives for the good purpose of redirecting us from this world to the next. The sixteenth-century Reformer John Calvin once wrote in a letter to a woman who had just recovered from serious illness:

> They [our illnesses] should serve us as medicine to purge us from worldly affections ... And since they are to us the messengers of death, we ought to learn to have one foot raised to take our departure when it shall please God.

A few years ago, I received a letter from missionary friends who were back "home" to receive medical help during a complicated pregnancy before returning to their work in a Muslim country. The husband wrote:

> It's been hard for [my wife] to be living in someone else's house and then think about having to pack everything up to leave the country two months after having a new baby. Please pray for [her] to be encouraged in the midst of the transition and pray that we all would have a better appreciation of heaven being our true home. Pray that we would long for God's kingdom.

Most of us are not missionaries, but we can think this way. Big changes in our life situation such as moving house, beginning a new job, or having a child often cause upheaval and inconvenience. These changes are never spiritually neutral. We may drift from God. Or we may draw closer as we trust him, remembering that this world is imperfect and we're made for a better one. Do the inconveniences in our lives send us into "fix-it mode," or do they encourage a longing for the world to come?

Finally, we should simply begin to live as though the new creation will come. We need consciously to decide to live out what we believe. There's a famous moment in the movie *Indiana Jones and the Holy Grail* when Indy needs to cross a deep chasm over a bridge he can't see. It's only in taking that first terrifying step onto the bridge that he can know it's there. Similarly, making decisions and sacrifices in light of the new creation assures us of its reality and superior value. This week, spend an hour doing something (helping a neighbor, reading the Bible, writing a poem, writing a check) you wouldn't do unless you believed that you're heading for a wonderful new creation. Jesus said that where our treasure is, our hearts will be also (Matthew 6 v 21). So, put money on your future. Your heart will follow.

Believing that the new creation is incredibly good (much better than now) and that through Christ it will certainly be ours (because it already is) makes us dissatisfied with the present and restless for the future. It's the balancing pole we need as we walk our tightrope, not falling off the wire into settling and despair.

The new creation is wonderful and certain

Content... ...with dissatisfaction

We're restless

We don't settle for now

We avoid despair

8. Patience

It's dangerous to urge Christians to greater restlessness.

The problem is that the wrong kind of restlessness leads to disaster. For those who don't hope in God's future and don't want to settle for a life of mild disappointment or outright despair, there is a popular option: try to seize it all now!

We all know how disappointing life can be. Maybe you never thought you'd still be single at age 35, or still stuck in an entry-level position, or still battling depression. The wrong kind of restlessness tells us that to be content in the present, we must be content *with* the present. So, if we're not content in the present, we need to change our present.

This kind of restlessness doesn't trust God's timing. It wants heaven now. But those who seek heaven on earth make it hell for everyone else. Parents who demand perfection crush their children. Employees who trample on anything and anyone to reach the top create toxic workplaces. Worse, when we're content with nothing less than heaven now, we're bound to disobey God in order to grab it. Attempting to walk into happiness, we stay far from God, or walk away from God. And that's (eternal) disaster.

So, while it's right to do so, it's dangerous to call for restlessness. We need to make sure we don't tip off the tightrope on the other side. We need to have patient restlessness. Restlessness with patience is Christian maturity. Restlessness without patience is disaster.

Our patience problem

Let's be honest. We live in an age that lacks patience! We're bombarded with the message that we can, should, must have everything now.

So we hate to wait. I once heard someone say if he's stuck in traffic, he turns his car around and drives the opposite direction—at least that way he's making good time. People in western cultures seem to move at a faster and faster pace. We believe "time is money," and we talk about it that way. We accumulate earned time, spend and save time, hate to waste it or lose it (after all, if this life is all there is, there's not much time to get everything done, to experience all we want to). We drink instant coffee, communicate with instant messaging and search the web with Google Instant. I had to admit my own ridiculous impatience when I found myself annoyed that a web search had taken longer than one second. Apparently, I'm not alone. It's been shown that if a website is more than 250 milliseconds slower than its competitor, it gets less traffic.

And the problem is that while we want fast, God likes slow. He really likes slow. His normal way of operating with people is to make them wait. God promised Abraham a son twenty-five years before Isaac was born. The nation of Israel waited hundreds of years in Egypt before being delivered, and thousands of years before receiving the promised Messiah-King. Before Jesus ascended to heaven, he commanded his followers to wait for the Holy Spirit. Do you see a pattern here?

We want fast, we're used to fast, but God likes slow... so we need to get used to slow. We get help in the book of James:

> Be patient, then, brothers and sisters, until the Lord's
> coming. See how the farmer waits for the land to yield its

valuable crop, patiently waiting for the autumn and spring rains. You too, be patient and stand firm, because the Lord's coming is near. Don't grumble against one another, brothers and sisters, or you will be judged. The Judge is standing at the door! Brothers and sisters, as an example of patience in the face of suffering, take the prophets who spoke in the name of the Lord. As you know, we count as blessed those who have persevered. You have heard of Job's perseverance and have seen what the Lord finally brought about. The Lord is full of compassion and mercy. (James 5 v 7-11)

Have it all, and have it now?

James' call to be patient for Jesus' return is a big challenge for most of us. Our general impatience in life (for traffic to move and websites to load) often translates into an unhealthy impatience for the new creation—unhealthy, because it's shot through with lack of trust in God's timing.

Years ago I received a booklet in the mail from a Christian ministry. Inside, on a detachable page, was printed a list of luxury cars (Ferrari, Mercedes, Porsche, Rolls Royce). If I indicated the car I wanted and sent in the form, this Christian ministry would pray I'd receive it. A drawing in the booklet summed up the promise they were making: a family stood beside a raging river. Over the river, like a bridge, lay a giant copy of the ministry's booklet, teaching the principles of how to be rich and healthy. On the other side of the river was a suburban home with a car in the driveway. The promise was clear: trust in God and you'll get it now! Cross over into a new life of prosperity.

There's a supposedly Christian movement that promises health and wealth in this life to followers of Jesus. If you have enough faith, God will give you houses, money, and cars. Here's an example of the message, quoted in December 2009's issue of the *Atlantic*: "We declare financial blessings! Financial miracles this week, NOW NOW NOW! ... More work! Better work! The best finances!" This message is preached on television and embraced by a good number of America's largest churches. In parts of Africa, it's the fastest-growing form of "Christianity."

Who wouldn't love this prosperity gospel? It says: *Don't wait for the new creation. Seize it all now.*

And I have to confess that I fall for it. I have opposed this gospel and sought to persuade others of its dangers; and yet I often construct my own mini-versions of it. In fact, I do so almost every day. My mini-prosperity gospels arise when I cultivate false expectations of what this present world can and should offer. When I begin a new day, my usual assumption is that things will go well for me. There will be ample food for breakfast, and enough hot water for my shower. My car will start. The people I meet during the day will understand and appreciate me. My neighbors will be friendly and will lend me their tools. My children will be well-behaved in the evening, be in bed on time, and will sleep well. When I'm on vacation, my expectations are ratcheted up even higher—woe betide the airline that dares cancel or delay my flight! I'm on vacation! I've waited and worked for this little slice of heaven on earth, and no one had better take it from me.

I can tell when my expectations are too high—when I'm trying to seize it all now—by noticing my reaction when something deviates from the plan. Am I annoyed at car trouble? Impatient with inefficiency? Grumpy when hungry? If something goes wrong, do I feel cheated? Am I angry with God, as though he hasn't delivered what he promised?

Despairing, because I didn't manage to take hold of the kind of day I need to be having right now?

If the answer to these questions is "Yes," then I'm not being patient enough. I'm not trusting God's timing. I'm trying to enjoy all his promised future in the present. I'm expecting perfection from an imperfect world. So I need to hear James' call for patience. In this life, bones will break, noses will run, traffic will snarl, and relationships will strain, all despite our own personal versions of the prosperity gospel.

Perhaps you've come to terms with how difficult this life can be for you. But it's more difficult not to expect heaven now for our children, isn't it? That's why so many parents provide their kids with a huge array of choices (sports to play, activities to enjoy, pets to own), while seeking to protect them from failure at all costs. We're telling our kids they can have, and ought to expect, heaven now. So when they taste failure, they don't know how to cope.

Don't get me wrong. It's not that we enjoy the hardships of life, or call evil good. I've wept with the parents of dead children and grieved with the husbands and wives of cheating spouses. It's also not that we're passive or lazy, never trying to improve things. But even in our worst circumstances and our boldest efforts to better the world, we accept God's timing that the new creation is not yet here. The Lord Jesus could have returned yesterday, or last year. He didn't. He's waiting, and so are we.

We see this in that passage in James, written to economically-deprived Christians. If James were a prosperity preacher, he would say: *Believe and you will receive! Have it now!* But he doesn't say that. Instead, he twice urges patience for the return of Jesus. Full deliverance and blessing will come—in the future. We wait patiently until then.

What does this mean in practice? Well, picture the man who always wished he could go to university—he loves to read and study, and college studies have been a long-held dream. Two years ago, he was offered a scholarship, but he's married with four kids now, and he knew pursuing a degree would require neglecting his family and mean he was never in church. He said no to the scholarship. That hurt, but he's okay with it. He knows he'll have forever to study God's words and works in the new creation, and he doesn't need to seize it all now.

Or imagine the woman who longed to be married, but somehow it never happened. There was a time in her late 30s when she hit it off with a guy she met at the gym. Everything went well for the first couple months, and then one night he pushed to have sex. When she said she wouldn't do that, he distanced himself, taking her dreams of marriage with him. That hurt, and still does, but she's okay with it. She knows she'll have forever to enjoy an intimate relationship with God and his people, and she doesn't need to seize it all now.

Patient trust in God and his timing makes us resilient and hopeful when life is hard. It's essential to avoiding disaster. If we're not patient, we'll become disillusioned when we get sickness and poverty (including relative poverty) instead of health and wealth. We'll fall away from Christ, thus losing the perfect health and wealth God promises us in the new creation. Trying to seize it all now, we'll lose it all then.

How can we be more patient?

How can we become more patient for our future, not seizing it all now? Thinking back to my engagement to Emma, two things fueled my patience. First, the engagement made me confident that the wedding was a definite go and the joys of marriage were assured. There was no need to try to seize ahead of time what was surely coming my way. Second, and as importantly, I was convinced Emma would be an amazing wife and my life would be much better as a married man. I was willing to wait as long as it took for the wedding day because I knew Emma was worth the wait. Wanting it then, I didn't try to seize it all ahead of time.

When we return to our passage in James, we can see that James appeals to both these things—the certainty and the greatness of our future—in order to strengthen patience. In other words, the same aspects of the new creation that prompt our restlessness also provide us with patience.

First, certainty. "Be patient and stand firm, because the Lord's coming is near ... The Judge is standing at the door!" (5 v 8-9). James isn't claiming to know exactly when Jesus will return. We know that Jesus' return could occur today, but we do not know that it will.

What's clear in James' words is that Jesus' return is absolutely certain. Therefore, we can wait patiently for it. We will never find that it will never happen, and look back with regret at opportunities we missed to seize more during this life.

Second, greatness. The farmer waits, and waits... and then reaps his "valuable crop." The prophets in Old Testament times kept going in hard times, waiting and waiting... and were "blessed." Job lost everything, suffering terribly, but "the Lord finally brought about" abundant provision (see Job 42 v 10-17). Their waiting was worth it! James' point is that ours will be, too.

Patience comes from knowing that God's future is ours and God's future is great. When we know it's sure, it can be slow. When we know it's great, we can wait.

Three tips

What are some practical ways to grow in patient waiting for the new creation?

First, we can ask God for help. Many of us never ask, because we think waiting is a passive activity rather than an active one. We think we can do it on our own. But Paul asked God to help Christians live with endurance and patience (Colossians 1 v 11). He said it is "through the Spirit" that we "eagerly await by faith the righteousness for which we hope" (Galatians 5 v 5). We can't do this on our own. Next time you're tempted to seize heaven now... pause... and pray for patience.

Second, we can practice waiting. God provides many opportunities in the daily situations of life to practice waiting (more often than we'd like!). Not long ago, I wheeled my cart into an Ikea checkout line, only to discover that the woman ahead of me had the most complicated order in the history of furniture-purchasing. The checkout clerk got on the phone, the minutes ticked by, and I experienced the ultimate checkout nightmare of watching people who had entered other lines after me now finished and walking away. My internal temperature began to rise. Then God reminded me he had a good purpose in this fifteen-minute wait, just as he has good purposes in my wait for the new creation. I asked myself: *If I can't trust God with fifteen minutes, how will I trust him with my life?*

Third, we can consider our waiting in light of the cross. During his life on earth, Jesus looked forward to his resurrection and return to heaven, speaking of it repeatedly to his disciples. But the cross demonstrates how very patient Jesus was. He knew his ascension had to come after his crucifixion. He was willing to wait, to trust that God's future would come in God's time. The cross therefore provides the perfect example of patience.

But thankfully, it does even more. It also provides forgiveness for our impatience. When we try to seize the new creation now, we're calling God's timing into question, implying he's less than fully wise. The cross provides forgiveness for this rebellion. The more we meditate on the cross, the more shallow appears any teaching that invites us to skip the suffering and grab the glory. That's not the way of Christ, so it's not going to be the way of the Christian. Our way is suffering now, glory then.

Settler, or seizer?

I'm closing in pretty hard on the age of 40, when many men have a "mid-life crisis." Some assess their lives and grow discouraged, realizing how little they've accomplished and how many of their dreams have gone and will go unfulfilled. Settling for now, they despair. They just get on with the life they have with a kind of quiet, unspoken desperation. Their lives go gray.

Others respond by dialing up the color, finding a young blonde and a red sports car and blue skies. They're trying to seize it all now. And in doing so they make a disaster of their relationships and of their own eternal future, throwing away the new creation for a new girlfriend.

These two mid-life responses may look very different—one lacks restlessness and the other lacks patience—but really, they're not so different. What they have in common is that they both ignore the new creation. That's a mistake we can all make, no matter our age. It's worth taking a moment to consider where you tend to be in the things we've talked about over the past three chapters.

Are there ways you settle for now, lacking restlessness? Do you get stuck in the difficulties of this life and get disappointed and then despairing? If so, get thinking about your future—get dissatisfied, yearning, leaning. God wants you up on tiptoe, not living flat-footed.

Are there ways you try to seize it all now, lacking patience (possibly even as you settle for now in other ways)? Are you heading for disaster because of a failure to trust God and his timing? Then get thinking about your future—it's so good and so certain, there's no need to seize it ahead of time.

Jesus is the only answer to our failures and the only hope for our growth. He'll help us make it safely across the tightrope. We don't need to settle for now or seize it all now, because Jesus beckons us from the perfect future he has already secured. With restless patience, we walk the wire toward him.

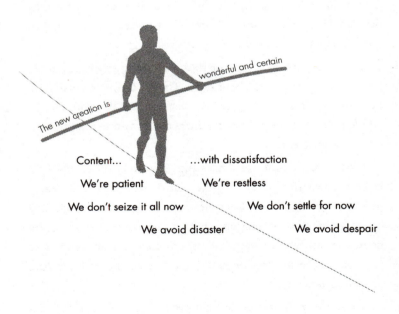

The new creation is wonderful and certain

Content... ...with dissatisfaction

We're patient We're restless

We don't seize it all now We don't settle for now

We avoid disaster We avoid despair

9. Heavenly citizens

I'm from a little town called Monson in the state of Maine. Monson has a population of 700; there's not much to it, and most people probably don't even notice it as they drive through. But I love Monson, because it's my hometown and it's familiar. I know the steepest hill for sledding in the winter, the best pizza place, and the friendliest people. I can show you the house I grew up in, the baseball field where I hit my one and only homerun, the lake where I failed my swim test (I ran aground doing the backstroke), and the dirt road where I almost jogged into a moose. Monson will always feel like home.

I've lived in a lot of other places since leaving Monson. In my late twenties, I spent four years studying in Cambridge, England. Living overseas was a great adventure. I loved the fish and chips, the self-deprecating English humor, the fact that some of the buildings were twice as old as my country, and all my wonderful English friends. But of course there were people and places and foods and traditions I missed from back home. Sometimes in England, I felt out of place and said embarrassing things—like when I told a friend I was getting too wet riding my bicycle in the rain and wanted to buy some waterproof pants (it turns out that in the UK pants are what Americans call underwear!).

One thing I really enjoyed in Cambridge was wandering along the walking paths that ran along the edges of the fields in the surrounding countryside. One afternoon, I walked toward the little village of Madingley, and stumbled upon something I wasn't expecting: home.

What I discovered was the Madingley American Cemetery. There I stood, looking out over 30 acres of beautifully maintained lawns and gardens, with gorgeous buildings and monuments, and thousands of white crosses marking the graves of American soldiers who died in World War II. As I walked among the graves, I felt a surge of enormous pride and patriotism and home-coming and homesickness all rolled together. Here I was, living in a far country, but suddenly experiencing a piece of the USA. In a sense, I was home. Yet it also reminded me that I had left home far behind. It made me remember that the USA is my country. It's where I was born and belong. I suddenly felt far from home.

Home, and far from home. That's meant to be the experience of each Christian in this world:

> Many live as enemies of the cross of Christ. Their destiny is destruction, their god is their stomach, and their glory is in their shame. Their mind is set on earthly things. But our citizenship is in heaven. And we eagerly await a Savior from there, the Lord Jesus Christ, who, by the power that enables him to bring everything under his control, will transform our lowly bodies so that they will be like his glorious body.
>
> (Philippians 3 v 18-21)

Paul is warning us against becoming people whose minds are set on earthly things. Why? Because a Christian's mind is, or should be, set on heaven; as he puts it, we "eagerly await a Savior" from there.

But Paul goes deeper than mind-set here; he goes to identity. "Our citizenship is in heaven." That means this world is not our home. Heaven is.

Where we belong

The new creation is our home. That sounds odd. In this life, Monson is my home because I grew up there and it's familiar to me. But God's people have never yet been to God's future, the new creation. Our home is a place we've never visited. How can it possibly be home?

It's home because it's where we most truly belong. We're going to live there for ever, much longer than the 80-90 years we'll hope to spend in this present life.

And it's home for a deeper reason. It's true that we have not yet come to the new creation. But it has come to us. Already in our lives as Christians we've begun to experience foretastes of our future. In a sense, we already know something of what it is like.

When Paul said Christians are citizens of heaven, he was writing to people living in Philippi, a Roman colony in Greece. Many residents of Philippi were citizens of Rome. They had special privileges and protections under Roman law. They were proud of their Roman identity. They cherished ties to their homeland, kept Roman customs, and obeyed Roman laws. Even though many of them would probably never have seen Rome, they lived like Romans.

Philippi was a mini Rome, a taste of Rome, though far from Rome. It's like my time in Madingley American Cemetery. It was a little bit of home, far from home.

God has already begun his work of new creation in this world, and his new creation work is... us! Whenever someone becomes a Christian, that is God's work of new creation—a work that will climax one day in the renewal of the entire universe. In 2 Corinthians 5 v 17, Paul says: "If anyone is in Christ, the new creation has come." Every local church is a little colony of God's new creation, just as Philippi was a colony of Rome.

This means a Christian isn't just the same old person doing new things. A Christian is a new person doing new things. When we trust in Jesus, our "hometown," our citizenship, our identity changes. It used to be this world. Now it's the new creation.

Home shapes our behavior

If the new creation is our new home, we'll behave in new ways. That's because we're shaped by where we're from.

Just think about how your own hometown has shaped you. I'm a product of Monson. The way I look at the world, interact with people, and even speak are shaped by growing up there. If I had adopted an English accent while living in Cambridge, I wouldn't have been living true to who I really am. For better or worse, I talk like a guy from Monson!

When we become citizens of heaven and our hometown changes, we change from the inside out. When we obey God, we're living in line with who we really are. And when we sin, we're out of line with who we really are. When a Christian sins, it's like an American switching on an English accent to fit in, or vice versa. Sure, an Englishman in New York or a Monson boy in Cambridge can do it; but it doesn't fit with who they really are.

Paul told the Philippians:

> Whatever happens, conduct yourselves in a manner worthy
> of the gospel of Christ.   (Philippians 1 v 27)

The word for "conduct yourselves" means to "live as a citizen."
Because we're citizens of the future heavenly kingdom, our
lives are to reflect the values, truth, and beauty of God's future.
The Roman citizens in Philippi lived like Romans. Christians
throughout this world, in thousands of cultures speaking
thousands of languages and with countless different accents,
are to live as citizens of the new creation.

When I saw the Madingley American Cemetery, I caught a
glimpse of America. When people saw Philippi, they caught
a glimpse of Rome. Christians are citizens of heaven. When
people see us, they should catch a glimpse of the greatness of
the new creation, the beauty of forever with God.

Life away from home

This means that Christians are home, and not yet home. We're
home and we're homesick, because the new creation is really
here in us, but not fully here in this world. We're restless
(homesick) and patient (OK with not yet being home).

In the meantime, on our way home, how do we live? It's the
question anyone moving overseas has to answer each day. *Where
do I go to buy milk? What will I do on my Saturday afternoons in this
place? Do I pay list price in the market, or am I supposed to haggle?*

The next two chapters of this book are about how to live as
restlessly patient citizens of heaven as we live in and interact
with this world. But here it is in a nutshell; restless patience
leads us to need this world less and love this world more.

That sounds a little contradictory. But a paradoxical way of life (restless patience) naturally produces a paradoxical effect (needing the world less and loving it more). Citizens of the world that is to come do not ignore or despise this world. Neither do they worship it. They are free from it, yet also fully for it.

Nik Wallenda's tightrope walk took him to an exhilarating place he'd never otherwise have been, a place none of us will ever be: 200 feet straight above Niagara Falls, in the mist and spray and wind. To get there, he had to walk the wire.

We'll see in the next two chapters that our freedom from this world produces marvelous inner transformation; and that our love for this world produces mighty outward action. By making us restlessly patient, God makes us both more joyful, and more productive. He changes both us, and our world.

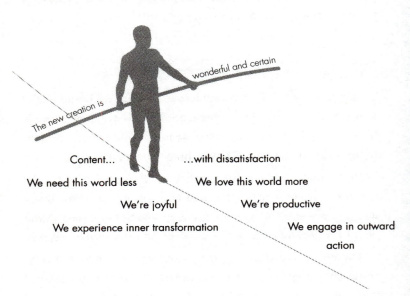

The new creation is wonderful and certain

Content... ...with dissatisfaction

We need this world less   We love this world more

We're joyful   We're productive

We experience inner transformation   We engage in outward action

10. Needing this world less

Restless patience for the new creation means we need this world less. Why?

Because this world is not the end of the story! There's something better coming our way. We don't settle into despair over everything we think is bad in our lives, and we don't seize disaster by trying to grab everything we think would be good for our lives.

I love Britain, but while living there I discovered a few things I wasn't crazy about. I encountered some odd foods (ever tried the Scottish delicacy, haggis?). I missed American customer service (in Britain, the customer is not always right; in fact, they are sometimes very, very wrong). At times I was lonely, and at other times I struggled under the pressure of succeeding in my graduate work.

Life in a different country was challenging. If I had been planning to stay in Britain for the rest of my life, I would have struggled more than I did. But my plan was to return to America in four years, so even the things I didn't like were all part of the adventure. They didn't bother me so much because I knew I would be returning home.

Of course, this is true for anyone living in a foreign country for a while. There's nothing intrinsically superior or inferior about the USA compared to Britain. My British friends find it off-putting when Americans confidently assert how good they are at something, and bizarre when American waitresses clear away plates while people are still eating! But if my British friends are simply on holiday in America for a couple weeks, they can regard these oddities with amusement rather than alarm.

It's the same for citizens of heaven. Knowing we have a future home steadies us in the present. As the new creation strengthens its hold, this world loosens its grip. We need it less. So, when it fails us, we don't fall apart. Better yet, our diminishing need for this world produces increasing fruit in our lives.

What difference does needing this world less make?

Endurance in suffering

We're all tempted to quit, all the time. The pile of unfinished books on my bedside table speaks eloquently to this. We'll quit anything—a strict diet, a tough exercise routine, a hard relationship. You name it, we'll quit it.

And when things get tough, we're tempted to quit trusting Jesus.

But restless patience helps us persevere through suffering. If forever is great and forever is mine, I can endure even though now is lousy.

We see this played out in what is likely the last letter Paul wrote, where he contrasts a quitter and a finisher:

> I have fought the good fight, I have finished the race, I have kept the faith. Now there is in store for me the crown of righteousness, which the Lord, the righteous Judge, will

award to me on that day—and not only to me, but also to all
who have longed for his appearing. Do your best to come
to me quickly, for Demas, because he loved this world, has
deserted me.   (2 Timothy 4 v 7-10)

Life is a fight. Life is a grueling race. How does Paul finish it?
How do we? By focusing on the future crown of righteousness;
by longing for our future with Jesus. Loving God's future helps
us last in the present.

Demas didn't last. He quit, deserting Paul and the gospel.
Why? "Because he loved this world." When we're in love with
now, we need it way too much to give it up. We give up on Jesus
instead. Loving a soft couch, we lose a future crown.

One of my heroes is Henry Martyn, who lived in the early
1800s. By the time he was 24, he had already distinguished
himself as a brilliant scholar. But he left behind a promising
career in order to pursue missionary work in India. Sailing
from England was bitterly difficult for him because he believed,
correctly, that he was leaving forever.

On Sunday, August 11, 1805, sailing along the south-west coast
of England, soon to pass out of view of his homeland, Martyn
preached on board his ship... and could barely stop himself from
breaking down in tears. He recounts movingly what this time
was like:

My anguish at times was inexpressible, when I awoke from
my disturbed dreams, to find myself actually on my way, with
a long sea rolling between me and all I held dear in this life.

To describe the variety of perplexing, heart-rending,
agonizing thoughts which passed through my mind, and
which, united with the weakness and languor of my body,
served to depress me into the depths of misery, would be
impossible.

What gave Martyn the strength to persevere? Why didn't he quit his plans, jump on another boat and sail straight home?

He persevered because his homesickness for heaven was greater than his homesickness for England. In that sermon, he had chosen Hebrews 11 v 16 as his text:

> They were longing for a better country—a heavenly one.
> Therefore God is not ashamed to be called their God, for he
> has prepared a city for them.

He wrote in his journal:

> In prayer I soon launched sweetly into eternity, and found
> joy unspeakable in thinking of my future rest, and of
> the boundless love and joy I should ever taste in Christ's
> beloved presence hereafter. I found no difficulty in stirring
> myself up to the contemplation of heaven; my soul through
> grace realized it, and I delighted to dwell by faith on those
> blissful scenes.

Martyn was restless for the new creation. He was patient, accepting hardship now instead of searching out a life of ease and comfort. He found "joy unspeakable in thinking of my future rest." He didn't need this world because he knew he was a citizen of a better one.

Henry Martyn died from fever six years later, far from England, still longing for the new creation. A few days before his death he wrote: "Oh, when shall time give place to eternity! When shall appear that new heaven and new earth wherein dwelleth righteousness!"

God may not call you to lose your home. But what if he calls you to lose some popularity for his sake? Or to lose a promotion? Or some comfort—a larger bonus, or just a quiet evening? If you need these things, you'll never give them up. But if you love the new creation, you won't need them. You'll be able to part with them. You'll persevere.

Jesus was willing to lose even his own life. He endured the cross "for the joy that was set before him" in eternity (Hebrews 12 v 2). For Jesus, a secure future meant a free present.

Regrets left behind

It would be nice to have some second chances in life. I'd learn guitar instead of trumpet. I wouldn't be so ungrateful toward my parents. I'd skip the badly misjudged haircut of my late teen years. Come to think of it, I might just skip my late teen years altogether.

There are other things I'd still like to do in this life. I want to read all the way through the bound set of fifty greatest works in Western literature that sits on my shelf (one volume down, 49 to go!). I have a dream my family will walk the Cumbria Way, a footpath through the English Lake District. I have a plan that each of my kids will learn an instrument and we'll form a hit bluegrass band (no, really!). My list goes on and on... and I realize increasingly that I won't be able to do all these things in my lifetime.

We all live with some regrets. When we make mistakes, it's natural to wish we hadn't. When we don't seize an opportunity, it's natural to wish we had.

But I've met people who are consumed with regret. Maybe you know parents who can't forgive themselves for the mistakes they made in raising their kids; spouses who can't get over their poor choice of a partner; graduates who dwell on their wasted college years, because they feel they worked too hard or didn't work hard enough; employees who believe they've squandered their lives at a dead-end, low-paying job when they might have had something so much better. Maybe you know people consumed with regret... or maybe you are that person.

If this world is all there is, if we settle for now, our regret over the bad mistakes and missed opportunities of our lives will dominate our lives. If we need this world, we can't bear to have squandered its potential. We spend our lives asking: "What if...?" and sighing: "If only..."

And it's restless patience that frees us from paralyzing regret.

When we become convinced that the new creation is superbly great and securely ours, we let go of our regret by taking hold of something better. We know that when we come to die, we won't have missed all our opportunities. For the follower of Jesus, death is the entrance to an even more satisfying experience of life.

So I don't need to be filled with regret over the bad things I've done and the good things I'll never do! In the new creation, I'll have time to read all I want. I'll walk the perfected version of the Cumbria Way (no litter, no mosquitoes)—or I'll walk on something even better than the Cumbria Way. I'll play some amazing bluegrass licks with my brother Ricky Skaggs. It's okay if we haven't traveled the world, possessed gorgeous looks, or achieved wild career success. This world isn't the whole story. There's another volume to come—and the sequel is better.

And it goes beyond even this. In the new creation, I will finally see that God was using the very sufferings, deprivations, and mistakes I most regretted to prepare me for forever. Paul says a seemingly bizarre thing in Philippians 1 v 29: "For it has been granted to you on behalf of Christ not only to believe in him, but also to suffer for him." The word translated "granted" here is the word for grace—undeserved kindness. Suffering is a kindness from God. Amazing! Only when we're patient, not trying to seize all our happiness now, will we be able to see that our hardships are not obstacles to the new creation—they are God's means of getting us there. God uses them to produce inner transformation.

This truth spares us from despair. Mistakes and missed opportunities no longer crush us.

Take a moment and think of a past mistake you really wish you hadn't made. Then think of a past opportunity you really wish you hadn't missed. The mistake might have been a big one, and the opportunity a great one—I'm not asking you to pretend otherwise. Got a couple in mind?

If you're a Christian, you'll be enjoying Jesus one million years from now. How does this knowledge affect the way you feel about your mistake, and about that missed opportunity?

One million years in the future, your mistake will be long past, but the character qualities God has worked in you through it (humility, reliance on him, hatred of sin) will be eternally present. Michelangelo's paintbrushes and chisels have long since passed out of this world—no one remembers them. But we all marvel at the amazing works of art they produced. God uses even the worst junk of our lives (which is temporary) to produce wonderful treasure (which is for ever). "For our light and momentary troubles are achieving for us an eternal glory that far outweighs them all" (2 Corinthians 4 v 17).

And that missed opportunity? In the new creation, there will be so many new and better opportunities to explore, you won't have the time to kick yourself for missing old ones.

You don't need to live a life of *what if* and *if only*. Instead, you can live asking "What next?"—because one day, the answer will be: *the new creation*.

Secure identity

Most of us are almost constantly seeking to establish our value in one way or another. I bet you've done it today.

We try to prove to others, or perhaps to ourselves, that we're worth respecting and loving. We often tie our value to what we've achieved in this life: the people we've known, the children we've raised, the jobs we've held, the skills we've honed.

Sometimes that works out well for us, because we manage to achieve a lot... so we feel, and other people agree, that we're valuable.

But the problem is that if we're resting on our resumé, and our resumé takes a hit (we lose a friend, or lose our job), so does our value. It's a risky strategy. Tying our value to our accomplishments is like tying a lifeboat to a sinking ship. Eventually, it's going to sink.

There's a better place for a Christian to find their value and identity, and it's (literally) out of this world. Remember who Paul tells us that we are as Christians, in Philippians 3? Citizens of heaven. That's where we belong. It's our home. That's who we are. It's our identity.

During my years in England, I never forgot I was an American. Sure, I ate English food, drank English tea, enjoyed English friends, suffered English weather, and watched English football. But I never thought I was English. I reminded myself of my identity by reading news from home and watching the Super Bowl once a year. I knew where I belonged (the US) and where I was soon going (the US).

This produced a deep sense of security in me. I didn't need to succeed in England in order to know who I was, or that I was loved. Back home I had all the friends and support I needed.

Even if every single person in all of England had hated me (I'm a nice enough guy, but it's theoretically possible), I wouldn't have despaired. Even if I had totally failed my graduate work (considerably more than theoretically possible), I would not have been totally crushed. Why? Because I knew two key things. First, my family and friends back home loved me; second, I was going home soon.

Citizens of heaven have stable identities. We know God loves us. And we know we're going home soon. Even if we fail by all standard measures in this life, we know we will be loved for ever in the life to come. Perhaps your children have rebelled, or your business has failed. Do you feel totally crushed and completely worthless? You don't need to. In the new creation, you will be loved for ever. And you'll soon be there.

There's another way the new creation gives us a secure identity—by showing us who we will one day be.

Think of a movie you've watched twice. On your second viewing, you evaluated the characters by what you knew of their future decisions and actions, right? You couldn't help reading the successful businessman back into the stammering child, the beautiful princess into the plain girl, or the nasty crook into the seemingly innocent boy. Who we are now is one part of the bigger picture that also includes who we'll be then. The meaning of our lives is determined by our whole lives, including our life beyond this life.

God's view of us is the one that counts, and God's view isn't limited to who we were in the past or are in the present. He knows us as we'll be for ever, in the new creation. He knows how much less annoying and how much more enjoyable a sin-free Stephen Witmer will be. He knows what my resurrection body will look like. It's going to be good! Our future, sinless selves are magnificent beyond what we can imagine, and God sees that already. It's an important piece of who we are. In fact, it's who we really are.

This helps us grasp our identity in Christ. Do you feel insignificant and worthless? Do you feel hopeless in your struggle with sin? If so, maybe you're not letting who you will be shape your view of who you are.

On the flip side, have you forgotten that you are different from the world around you? Have you forgotten that you don't fully belong here? Maybe you need to remember you're a citizen of heaven.

The joy of heavenly citizenship

Restlessly patient people are unusually joyful. We experience the hard stuff of this life, and we know it's preparing us for forever. We enjoy the good stuff of this life, and remember it's a mere foretaste of forever. And whether life is hard, or good, or a mixture, it is all getting us closer to forever. God is causing all things to work together for our good, and is moving us toward our final goal. We don't fall away in suffering, we don't fall apart with regret, and we don't fall into the trap of defining ourselves only by who we presently are.

The great paradox is that it's as we see this world as only part of the story, not the whole story, that we're liberated to enjoy this brief portion of it. It's as we need this world less that we can enjoy it more.

11. Loving this world more

A few years ago, our toddler stuffed some coins into the CD player of our Honda Civic. Because it was a CD player and not a piggy bank, it broke. And because I am a skinflint, I suffered through a year of music-less driving. But eventually, I caved in. I knew what kind of CD player I needed; I knew where to get one; so I paid my money, and suddenly there was music again. It was great!

But only for a month. The music ended when we were rear-ended. We were OK, but the car was wrecked, bound for a junkyard. A few days later, I went to collect our stuff from the car. I sat there in the driver's seat saying goodbye and staring ruefully at the CD player I had paid good money for, just a month earlier.

What makes us decide to invest in something in order to improve it? First, we need to care enough to want to improve it. Second, we need to have some confidence that the thing we improve will last long enough for the improvement to matter. Third, we need to have a clear idea of what improvement actually looks like.

And that leads us to a problem when we look at our world—both the planet, and the people in it. It's beautiful, but it's also very broken. Hurricanes and tsunamis bring devastation, droughts destroy crops, and fires rage. Governments are often corrupt, education is often ineffective, and there are huge inequalities between rich and poor. Our neighbors are unlikeable gossips, our co-workers are difficult, our kids seem to be going off the rails.

The brokenness of this world is why it needs fixing. But it's also what keeps us from wanting to fix it. It hurts us, so we withdraw. Its problems intimidate us, and we feel overwhelmed. It's easier just to watch more television.

If we're to invest productively in this broken world, we need help. And we find help by looking to the world to come. Caring deeply about the new creation does not make us no earthly good; it makes us more earthly good.

That's because restless patience gives us exactly the three things we need for productive work here and now. It motivates us to want to improve our world; it shows us the stunning significance of our work in it; and it tells us how to improve it.

The urge to improve

In his letters, Paul almost always joins a command to a motivation. For instance, here's a command:

> Let no debt remain outstanding, except the continuing debt
> to love one another, for whoever loves others has fulfilled
> the law.   (Romans 13 v 8)

This is a command to love everyone, not just fellow Christians. "Others" means not just people in general, but the specific people God brings into my life for me to help. Whoever is right in front of me—I'm to love them.

It's easy to "love humanity" from a comfortable armchair. But loving particular people—Veronica, who needs rent money; Joe, who can't get out of his house—requires active involvement and sacrifice. Loving people different from me—Ajith, who worships a different god; Franklin, who thinks any belief in God is absurd—requires humility and commitment. Yet as Jesus showed in the parable of the Good Samaritan, this is exactly what it means to love our neighbor.

That's the command; what's the motivation Paul gives?

> And do this, understanding the present time. (v 11)

It isn't immediately clear how this is a motivation! What exactly do we need to understand about the present time, and why does it fuel love? Paul continues:

> The hour has already come for you to wake up from your slumber, because our salvation is nearer now than when we first believed. The night is nearly over; the day is almost here. So let us put aside the deeds of darkness and put on the armor of light. Let us behave decently, as in the daytime. (v 11-13)

The "day" is the return of Jesus, the day of our final salvation, which ushers in the new creation. The "night" is this present age. So Paul is saying: *Look at the time! The night is nearly over; the day is almost here.*

Paul's point is that the new creation is very close, and therefore we should begin living now according to its values.

Whenever I'm returning home from traveling overseas, I get back into sync with home as the plane nears the airport: I change my watch to local time, find the keys to my car and my house, and make sure I have some US dollars in my wallet. That's what Paul is telling us to do. Home is almost here. It's close enough to see. And it is a world of astonishing love. Love "never fails";

it "remains" (1 Corinthians 13 v 8, 13). Love continues from this world into the next. It lasts for ever. As the New Testament scholar N.T. Wright says in *The Resurrection of the Son of God*: "Love is not merely the Christian duty, it is also the Christian destiny." Therefore, to get in sync with the new creation means to start loving those around us. It's what we'll do forever... and forever is already breaking into our present.

Don't miss what this means: living as a citizen of heaven means loving others on earth! The more we lean toward the world to come, the more we love this world.

Love is the rocket fuel for amazing productivity in this world. We protect the environment as an act of love toward those who share it with us, and toward future generations. Love drives us to work for prison reform, tutor underprivileged kids, fight for the lives of the unborn. And above all, love sends us with the gospel across the ocean to Nepal, or across the street to our neighbor.

The world is an intimidatingly big and broken place. How to fix it? Paul says start with "the other." We love and serve our world one person at a time. These acts of love may seem small and insignificant, but they're not. It's a miracle whenever unlovely things and unlovely people are loved with heavenly love. As citizens of heaven extend the love of the new creation into the here and now, this world sees a better world to come.

The world is worth improving

I loved that Honda Civic. But if I'd known I'd lose it in a month, I would never have invested in improving it. So, what about this world? Will it last? Is it worth improving?

The first and most important answer is: human beings are part of this world, and they last forever. Death is a comma, not a period; we all live from this world into the next. Each of us is on our way to an unimaginably great or unspeakably bad future. Remember Jesus' words: "All who are in their graves will hear [my] voice and come out." Some will rise "to live," others "to be condemned" (John 5 v 28-29).

The best way to improve this world is to share and spread the gospel of Jesus Christ. Why? Because love seeks to meet the needs of this world and to relieve its suffering. And love recognizes that the greatest need is eternal life, and the greatest suffering is eternal hell. Only the gospel can meet that need and relieve that suffering. It is a wonderful thing to bring a foretaste of the new creation to someone by crafting a poem, drafting a just law, or righting a wrong. It is even more wonderful to bring that person into the new creation, forever. Loving this world often involves much more than sharing the gospel; but it cannot mean less than seeking to share the gospel.

But is it worth working to improve the world in other ways? What about creation care, or working to eradicate diseases, or address social problems?

One view is that, since God intends to destroy this present world and create a brand new one, we can cut down the rain forests and pollute the environment; or, on a smaller scale, jump in the car when we could walk or drop litter when the trash-can isn't easily at hand. God will trash this world, so we can trash it ourselves. It's dubious logic; but the real problem is in the premise. In Chapter Two, we saw that God's plan is not to discard this present world, but to renew it. The world we're heading to is the world we're living in... but liberated, renewed and perfected. It will be radically different, unimaginably better, and yet still this world. So the direction of this world is toward perfection; we can either work in that direction, or work against it.

But this raises another question. If God really does plan to perfect this world (planet and people), why should we waste our time and effort trying to improve it now? God's going to get the job done anyway, and he'll do it much better than we can. If I had been told that my local mechanic was soon going to rebuild and refurbish my car as a birthday present to me, I certainly wouldn't have bought a new CD player. God will make us sinless in the new creation, so why struggle against sin now? Does it really make sense to improve what God will perfect?

The Bible offers us a number of important reasons to invest in this world. We are to aim to please God and bring him glory by obeying him. God wants his people to steward and manage the earth and all that fills it (see Genesis 1 v 26-28 and Psalm 8). He wants us to help the poor and afflicted in society (see Isaiah 58). Moreover, we're called to live like Christ, who himself cared for the poor, sick, and marginalized during his earthly ministry.

These are great reasons to invest productively in this world. The new creation gives us an additional motivation—an important and oft-forgotten one. Although the Bible never tells us exactly how the work we do in and for this world will carry over to the next, I believe there are suggestions that somehow it will. That is, our improvements now are part of God's plan to recreate the world, not irrelevant to that plan. We're dealing here with hints and clues and suppositions, so we can't be certain; but they're really important hints that point in a common direction.

When we read the descriptions of the resurrected Jesus in the four Gospels, we get a glimpse of the new creation. Jesus' resurrection body is like the resurrection bodies we'll have one day. It's like a piece of the future visiting the present, a clue of what that future will be like. And the resurrected Jesus is still

Jesus. He says to his disciples: "It is I myself!" (Luke 24 v 39). He recognizes his friends and treats them with the affection he cultivated over their years together. He remembers things he knew before his resurrection, such as Peter's denial. He bears marks from the cross in his resurrection flesh.

There's no reason to think it will be different for Christians. The people we become during our earthly lives will continue on into who we are forever in the new creation. Yes, I'll be a better Stephen, but I won't become a Stuart or a Steffan—I'll still be Stephen. The fact that I'll still be me suggests that in some way the character and skills I develop in this life will endure into the life to come. If that's true, it's worthwhile cultivating thankfulness, and memorizing a psalm. And, if it will help me grow in godliness or develop my gifts, it is worth learning to play a musical instrument or picking up a sport. It's also worth taking the time and effort to help other Christians grow and flourish in this life, since they'll still be "them" in the life to come. Yes, if we are trusting in Jesus and have been justified by faith, God will perfect us—but he will perfect *us*, the people we've become in this life.

What's true of us as individuals also seems to be true of human societies. A glimpse into the life beyond this one shows that there are still recognizable nations, tribes, peoples, and languages.

> After this I looked, and there before me was a great
> multitude that no one could count, from every nation, tribe,
> people and language, standing before the throne and before
> the Lamb. (Revelation 7 v 9)

> By [the light of the glory of God] will the nations walk, and
> the kings of the earth will bring their glory into [the new
> Jerusalem] ... They will bring into it the glory and the honor
> of the nations. (Revelation 21 v 24, 26)

As author Randy Alcorn says in his book *Heaven*, the nations and kings will: "bring into the new world a national and personal history, an ethnic identity, and a wealth of customs, art forms, and knowledge." God renews and perfects but does not obliterate culture. If that's true, it's worth working to improve society by serving a prickly neighbor, trying to reduce gang violence in your neighborhood, volunteering at a soup kitchen, drafting a better law, or painting a still life. What we do now matters.

It's the same with the earth itself. The earth we improve now is the earth God will perfect then. This suggests it is worth saving a species, or picking up trash on your block, or reducing habits that waste natural resources. Not because God can't do it anyway, but because then we get to be part of what God is doing and will do. What we do now matters.

A year ago, I was painting a piece of furniture, and I let my son help. He made a royal mess of it. As I worked around him, I took his messy efforts and improved them, often spreading and smoothing the globs of paint he had spattered on. Though his work wasn't great, it mattered. It became part of the finished product. He can point to that furniture and truthfully say: "I helped paint that." Somehow, God includes our modest efforts, done in his service, within his mighty transformation of the world. Working for positive change in this world is not pointless. It is worthwhile. What we do now matters.

We know how to make improvements

Lots of people who don't love or believe in God nonetheless love this world and work with remarkable industry and commitment to improve it.

And often their work makes this world a better place in the here and now. Think of the atheists who took part in the Civil Rights marches of the 1960s. Or your kindly, non-Christian neighbor who cuts the grass of an elderly widow every week. Or the many secular people who volunteer in schools, prisons, libraries, and hospitals. Christians don't have a monopoly on doing good; in fact, I sometimes think I should be more challenged by the actions of those around me who don't have the motivations I enjoy as a Christian.

But sometimes their work makes the world worse. There are well-meaning people who tirelessly devote their lives to promoting causes they think will improve things—abortion on demand, the redefinition of sexual ethics—that aren't in line with God's plans for his world, and won't be part of the world in eternity. Others work toward an end that will make the world a better place in one way, but they pursue it using means that make the world a worse place in a different way. Radical environmental groups aim to protect the planet (good goal) through arson or bombing (bad means).

The point is, unless we know the right goal (God's goal) and the right means (God's means), our efforts at positive change will be hit or miss. Sometimes they'll happen to be right, but other times they'll be dead wrong.

Christians are in the unique position of wanting to help the world and knowing how it can be helped. We have an agenda for change, because God has shown us his. He will transform his followers into the image of Jesus. And he will remake this present cosmos into the new creation. All of which means that God's perfect future kingdom, which lies in our future and which we have seen embodied in his King, Jesus, is our blueprint for change.

Christ doesn't change, nor does God's plan for the new creation. So our goal is fixed and stable. And that puts us in a position to make progress. The twentieth-century writer, G.K. Chesterton, illustrated this in his book *Orthodoxy* by imagining a man who wants an entirely blue world—and who therefore does his best to paint the whole world blue. He has heroic adventures, for instance: "the putting of the last touches to a blue tiger."

His progress is slow, but as long as his goal of a blue world remains constant, he will nevertheless make progress. However, if he alters his color of preference frequently, deciding he actually needs to paint the world red, yellow, or purple, he will make no progress at all. Equally, if we change our ideas about what heaven-on-earth (whether God-ruled or secular) is like, we'll never be able to make a difference, as Chesterton points out:

> As long as the vision of heaven is always changing, the vision of earth will be exactly the same. No ideal will remain long enough to be realized, or even partly realized ... Man will never change his environment; for he will always change his mind.

We need a stable goal... and we need the right means for achieving that goal. To return to Chesterton's image, it may be good to have a blue world, but if you're killing squirrels so you can use their tails as paintbrushes, it will not be a good blue world. And so the Bible, in telling us what the new creation is like, and showing us what it looks like in Jesus, and in telling us how to live in this world, tells us what ends to pursue, and what means to use. Our efforts cannot be in vain, and they will not be compromised. We can be amazingly productive.

The productivity of heavenly citizenship

C.S. Lewis was right:

> If you read history you will find that the Christians who
> did most for the present world were precisely those who
> thought most of the next ... It is since Christians have largely
> ceased to think of the other world that they have become so
> ineffective in this.

Do you "think of the other world"? The more you do, the more good you'll do in and for this one. Are you loving this world? Are you working productively in it? I can't say what this will look like in your life, but it will look like *something*. Restless patience for the future starts inside us, but never stays there—it always flows outward in practical deeds of love for our neighborhoods and the nations.

Maybe as you fall more and more in love with your heavenly home, you'll be moved to show and share the gospel by starting a conversation about Christ with a co-worker, or by volunteering for your church's nursing-home ministry, or by joining the campaign against sex trafficking. If you're restlessly patient, it's going to come out somehow!

12. Restless patience

It's a gorgeous summer day in Massachusetts. The sun's warmth is on my shoulders and the breeze is stirring the trees overhead. I'm sitting in a chair in my backyard by the gigantic sandbox I built a few weeks ago. As I watch my son making sandcastles, I can hear my daughter splashing in the plastic pool behind me and chattering to my wife.

I feel blessed. God has given me so much. And then the thought crosses my mind: this near-perfect moment is just a foretaste. All the good things I have are just glimmers of where I'm heading. If I'm experiencing this kind of beauty in a fallen world, what pleasures will there be in the new creation that Jesus died to open up to me and will return to bring to me? *Come, Lord Jesus!*

I begin to lean forward—not physically in my chair, but inwardly in my heart. Blessedness now makes me restlessly patient for total blessedness then.

Of course, this present moment won't last. Our family life isn't perfect (early this morning both kids were awake early and whining, and I was responding with anger and impatience). For the time being, there is no grabbing, pinching, yelling, screaming, slapping, poking, or kicking—but I'd give it about three minutes.

And even as I sit here in the sun, all is not well. I think of a difficult pastoral issue that puzzles and grieves me and must be addressed. I know that right now, there are many people—some of whom I know—who have never, and likely will never in this life, enjoy what I'm experiencing right now. And I can't forget the friend I tried to help and wound up hurting... and who won't forgive me. There is brokenness in my life. I've been wronged, and I've wronged others. I sin and ache and cry and fear and envy. There's hurt within and all around me. *Come, Lord Jesus!*

As I consider these things I once again begin to lean forward. Blessedness was pulling me forward. Now brokenness is pushing me.

Come, Lord Jesus! Bring the wholeness and peace for which we all long! Change me now to be ready for my future. Help me to know that your return is my future. Give me patience to wait, and restlessness till it comes. Help me, each day, to be both realistic and optimistic—when I suffer, to be neither overly surprised nor overwhelmed. Don't let me expect too much in the present or hope for too little in the future. Remind me that life is hard, but there will be healing. Keep my feet planted and my heart buoyant.

Sitting here beside the sandbox, there's a tug and a push within my heart. This world is not my home. It's making claims on me every day, asking me to place its concerns and priorities first. But I can't do that. I'm a citizen of heaven. What matters most to me as I sit here experiencing blessedness and brokenness is that I make it to my future home and that my family and my church and my friends and my neighbors come with me.

I won't settle for the blessings of now; the future holds even more. I won't despair about the brokenness of now; the future holds none of these things. For now, I want to be patiently restless. But I know that one day soon my restlessness will give way to perfect rest. And I won't need patience anymore, because I'll have what I've waited for.

> They desire a better country, that is, a heavenly one.
> Therefore God is not ashamed to be called their God, for he
> has prepared for them a city. (Hebrews 11 v 16, ESV)

Come, Lord Jesus!

The future of this world is wonderful, and certain. If you trust in Christ, your future is wonderful, and certain. You need not settle for now and despair, or try to seize it all now and cause disaster. You can need this world less, and love it more. You can lean forward in the best of times, and lean forward in the worst of times. You can enjoy walking the tightrope of restlessness and patience, getting ever closer to home.

> Christ, having been offered once to bear the sins of many, will
> appear a second time, not to deal with sin but to save those
> who are eagerly waiting for him. (Hebrews 9 v 28, ESV)

Come, Lord Jesus!

Bibliography

Heaven, Randy Alcorn (Tyndale House Publishers)

A Foot in Two Worlds, John Chapman (Matthias Media)

Orthodoxy: The Romance of Faith, G.K. Chesterton (Moody Press)

Mere Christianity, C.S. Lewis (Harper in the US / William Collins in the UK)

God is the Gospel: Meditations on God's Love as the Gift of Himself, John Piper (published by Crossway / IVP UK)

The Resurrection of the Son of God, N.T. Wright (Fortress Press / SPCK)

Thank you...

...to the people of Pepperell Christian Fellowship, for loving me and my family, and allowing me the great privilege of shepherding you and teaching you the Bible. To my fellow elders: thanks, guys, for giving me time away to write this book and for being such faithful partners in the gospel.

...to David Wells, Collin Hansen, Dennis Hollinger, and Kyle Lammott, for reading draft chapters; and to students at the University of Manchester and Harvard University, and my friends at the Center for Pastor Theologians and the Gospel Alliance, for hearing and discussing these ideas with me.

...to Carl Laferton, my editor at The Good Book Company, who has taught me a lot about writing and become a good friend in the process. I'm thankful to God for you, Carl.

...to the good folks at the Blackbird Café in Groton, Massachusetts, and Café Smart in Belfast, Northern Ireland, where a good amount of the writing was done.

...to my grandparents, Eugene and Anne, for your faithful witness to the reality and importance of the new creation; to my parents, Daryl and Mary, for giving me a love for the Bible and a confidence in what it says about our future.

...to my three children, Samuel, Annie, and Henry: you bring me great joy!

...and most of all to my wife, Emma, who has lived with this book as long as she's lived with me, and has cheerfully freed me to write it. Emma, you point me to Jesus more than anyone else, and I love you.

Other books in the **How to** series

Serving without sinking

John Hindley

This book shows what happens in our hearts as we do "Christian serving," and why we so easily see our service as a burden and duty. It points us back to the greatest Servant of all, and utterly reshapes our view of ourselves so that we can serve long, hard, sacrificially... and joyfully.

"One of the best books of the year."
Christopher Ash, Director of
Cornhill Training Course, London

"It has been a joy to recommend this book—it will be a great blessing to you."
Tim Challies, pastor and blogger

"This will transform the way you think about serving Jesus. I wish I'd read this twenty years ago—buy it, read it, give it!"
Carrie Sandom, author of "Different By Design"

Look out for...

- **Compared to her:** How to experience real contentment
  by Sophie de Witt

- **A City with walls:** How to be a man of self-control
  by Dai Hankey Launching fall 2014

- **The heart of singleness:** How to be single and satisfied
  (for women) *by Andrea Trevenna*

Order from your local Good Book website:

UK & Europe: www.thegoodbook.co.uk • US & Canada: www.thegoodbook.com
Australia: www.thegoodbook.com.au • New Zealand: www.thegoodbook.co.nz

Also available from **thegoodbook** COMPANY

PASSION

HOW CHRIST'S FINAL DAY
CHANGES YOUR EVERY DAY

The cross of Jesus is the centre of human history, and the centre of the Christian faith. And so it should dominate our view of ourselves, our future... and our present.

But does it? And how should it? Mike McKinley follows Luke's account of the final day of Jesus Christ's life on earth. See the hope and the anguish; the joy and the pain; the treachery, desertion, torture and the final heartbreaking, lifebringing death.

Whether you are exploring Christianity, new to faith, or have been following Jesus for years, discover how Christ's Passion changes your heart and challenges your life, transforming not just your last day, but your every day.

Mike McKinley is pastor of Guilford Baptist Church in Virginia, and the author of *"Did the devil make me do it?"* and *"Am I really a Christian?"*

"A gripping, heartwarming read"
William Taylor, Rector of St Helen's Bishopsgate, London

thegoodbook
COMPANY

Opening up the Bible

At The Good Book Company, we are dedicated to helping Christians and local churches grow. We believe that God's growth process always starts with hearing clearly what he has said to us through his timeless word—the Bible.

Ever since we opened our doors in 1991, we have been striving to produce resources that honor God in the way the Bible is used. We have grown to become an international provider of user-friendly resources to the Christian community, with believers of all backgrounds and denominations using our Bible studies, books, evangelistic resources, DVD-based courses and training events.

We want to equip ordinary Christians to live for Christ day by day, and churches to grow in their knowledge of God, their love for one another, and the effectiveness of their outreach.

Call us for a discussion of your needs or visit one of our local websites for more information on the resources and services we provide.

US & Canada: www.thegoodbook.com
UK & Europe: www.thegoodbook.co.uk
Australia: www.thegoodbook.com.au
New Zealand: www.thegoodbook.co.nz

US & Canada: 866 244 2165
UK & Europe: 0333 123 0880
Australia: (02) 6100 4211
New Zealand (+64) 3 343 1990

www.christianityexplored.org

Our partner site is a great place for those exploring the Christian faith, with a clear explanation of the good news, powerful testimonies and answers to difficult questions.

One life. What's it all about?